NEW DIRECTIONS FOR INSTITUTIONAL RESEARCH

J. Fredericks Volkwein, *State University of New York at Albany*
EDITOR-IN-CHIEF

Larry H. Litten, *Consortium on Financing Higher Education, Cambridge, Massachusetts*
ASSOCIATE EDITOR

Assessing Graduate and Professional Education: Current Realities, Future Prospects

Jennifer Grant Haworth
Loyola University Chicago

EDITOR

Number 92, Winter 1996

JOSSEY-BASS PUBLISHERS
San Francisco

ASSESSING GRADUATE AND PROFESSIONAL EDUCATION: CURRENT
REALITIES, FUTURE PROSPECTS
Jennifer Grant Haworth (ed.)
New Directions for Institutional Research, no. 92
Volume XVIII, Number 4
J. Fredericks Volkwein, Editor-in-Chief

Microfilm copies of issues and articles are available in 16mm and 35mm,
as well as microfiche in 105mm, through University Microfilms Inc., 300
North Zeeb Road, Ann Arbor, Michigan 48106-1346.

ISSN 0271-0579   ISBN 0-7879-9899-0

NEW DIRECTIONS FOR INSTITUTIONAL RESEARCH is part of The Jossey-Bass
Higher and Adult Education Series and is published quarterly by Jossey-
Bass Inc., Publishers, 350 Sansome Street, San Francisco, California
94104-1342 (publication number USPS 098-830). Periodicals postage
paid at San Francisco, California, and at additional mailing offices. POST-
MASTER: Send address changes to New Directions for Institutional Re-
search, Jossey-Bass Inc., Publishers, 350 Sansome Street, San Francisco,
California 94104-1342.

SUBSCRIPTIONS cost $52.00 for individuals and $79.00 for institutions,
agencies, and libraries.

EDITORIAL CORRESPONDENCE should be sent to J. Fredericks Volkwein,
Institutional Research, Administration 241, State University of New York
at Albany, Albany, NY 12222.

Photograph of the library by Michael Graves at San Juan Capistrano by
Chad Slattery © 1984. All rights reserved.

Manufactured in the United States of America on Lyons Falls
Pathfinder Tradebook. This paper is acid-free and 100 percent
totally chlorine-free.

THE ASSOCIATION FOR INSTITUTIONAL RESEARCH was created in 1966 to benefit, assist, and advance research leading to improved understanding, planning, and operation of institutions of higher education. Publication policy is set by its Publications Board.

For information about the Association for Institutional Research, write to the following address:

AIR Executive Office
114 Stone Building
Florida State University
Tallahassee, FL 32306-3038

(904) 644-4470

CONTENTS

EDITOR'S NOTES

Over the past decade, the so-called "assessment movement" has taken American higher education by storm. In one state after another, legislators have put the accountability squeeze on public colleges and universities, requiring them to implement assessment programs aimed at documenting institutional effectiveness and student achievement (Davis, 1989; Ewell, in Stark and Thomas, 1994). Many major accrediting bodies have followed suit, emphasizing the assessment of student achievement as an important criterion in the accrediting process.

Administrators and others have responded to these pressures by establishing campus-based assessment offices, creating faculty development programs to acquaint faculty with various assessment methods, and implementing campus-wide efforts to study and document student learning outcomes.

Interestingly, despite its burgeoning popularity, the recent assessment movement has focused largely on undergraduate education. The vast majority of studies, reports, and writings in the literature concentrate on undergraduate education and student achievement, leaving institutional researchers, administrators, and faculty with scant information on the scope, practice, or impact of assessment in graduate education. This is a particularly curious and serious omission for at least two reasons.

First, over the past three decades, the demand for graduate and professional education in this country has skyrocketed. Between 1960 and 1993, for example, the number of master's degrees awarded annually nearly quadrupled, from less than 75,000 in 1960 to more than 369,000 in 1993. A similar phenomenon occurred in doctoral education. The number of doctoral degrees awarded annually rose from approximately 15,000 in the early 1970s to more than 42,000 in the mid-1990s. The number of first-professional degrees conferred in dentistry, medicine, and law also increased dramatically, nearly tripling in number between 1960 and 1993 (from 19,519 to 59,438 degrees) (National Center for Education Statistics, 1995; *Chronicle of Higher Education*, 1995). Forecasters predict that student and employer demand for graduate education—particularly in the professions but also in applied fields of study at the master's level—will continue to grow, as the information and high-technology revolution in the United States extends into the foreseeable future (National Center for Education Statistics, 1991). Such an expansion demands that educators devote more attention to the quality of advanced-degree programs in this country, particularly in terms of assessing the range of effects they have on students.

Second, there has been growing dissatisfaction in both the public and private sectors that our nation's graduate and professional schools are failing to prepare individuals adequately for the changing demands of the workplace.

Employers, in particular, have raised serious concerns about the often poorly developed written and verbal communication skills, as well as interpersonal skills, of many advanced-degree recipients. Administrators and faculty have often been at a loss to respond to these criticisms, in large measure because they (and others) have not systematically examined student outcomes at the graduate level. With pressures for accountability and questions about quality looming, there is a strong need for institutional researchers, administrators, and faculty to assess the impact that graduate study has on students, as well as to examine and document how various processes within these programs contribute to various outcomes, ranging from students' knowledge and skills development to program completion rates.

Acknowledging the need to draw more attention to and increase the use of assessment in graduate and professional education, I have carved out two purposes for this volume. The first is to provide institutional researchers, administrators, and faculty with a familiarity of the research and writing on assessment in graduate and professional programs, particularly as it relates to various outcomes measures. The second purpose is to provide these same audiences with practical information on various methods and strategies for assessing and improving advanced-degree programs on their own campuses.

Given these major purposes, the volume is organized into three sections. The first section consists of a single chapter. In Chapter One, Anne E. Bilder and Clifton F. Conrad set a tone for the volume, noting the dearth of literature on assessment at the graduate level. Seeing this as an opportunity rather than an obstacle, Bilder and Conrad raise several challenges that institutional researchers, administrators, and faculty should consider before undertaking student outcome assessment studies. Among others, these include the need to determine the purposes of assessment, to define clearly what outcomes will be assessed, and to establish how assessment results will be used.

The second section focuses on specific assessment arenas relevant to graduate and professional education. In Chapter Two, Peter D. Syverson provides an overview of the changes in demand that have occurred in advanced-degree programs over the past twenty-five years and offers insights into how institutional researchers and others can monitor such changes on their own campuses. In Chapter Three, Linda Serra Hagedorn and Amaury Nora draw on various studies in the literature to evaluate how well conventional graduate admissions criteria predict student achievement. They then offer an alternative framework for understanding and assessing student success in advanced-degree programs. In Chapter Four, Jennifer Grant Haworth and Clifton F. Conrad explore the ever-popular issue of quality in graduate education. Drawing on data from a national study of master's education, Haworth and Conrad present a theory of program quality that refocuses quality assessment on various program processes and resources (human and otherwise) that contribute significantly to student learning. Maresi Nerad and Debra Sands Miller conclude this section by describing their recent research on graduate student retention at the University of California, Berkeley. In addition to providing information on the methods they used to study and assess retention, Nerad and Miller highlight several factors that contribute to student attrition (primarily at the doctoral level) and offer a number of recommendations aimed at improving graduate student completion rates.

The last section provides institutional researchers, administrators, and faculty with several suggestions for researching various outcomes in advanced-degree programs. In Chapter Six, Leonard L. Baird provides a framework for assessing student learning outcomes in graduate and professional programs and discusses various methods that can be used to accomplish this purpose. Finally, in Chapter Seven, Jennifer Grant Haworth summarizes the major themes of the volume. She offers her observations on the current state of assessment in graduate (and, to a lesser extent, professional) education and concludes with an agenda for future research in this area.

In the late 1980s, Derek Bok encouraged faculty and administrators in his book, *Higher Learning,* to study the learning process and assess the effects of its programs. At the undergraduate level, Bok's suggestion has been heard and, increasingly, followed. It is my hope that the same will occur in graduate and professional education. This volume is a beginning step in that direction.

This volume is intended to advance the practice of assessment in graduate and professional education. It is not the last word in a rapidly developing field, however, so we have established a means of carrying on an electronic discussion of assessment issues raised herein. We have established an electronic discussion group (a listserv), which will remain in operation for a year from the publication of this volume. To participate in this discussion send an e-mail message to: listserv@mitvma.mit.edu. The text of your e-mail should say: subscribe NDIRgrad [firstname] [lastname]. Substitute your two names in the bracketed spaces without including the brackets. Leave the subject line of your message blank, and if you have an automatic signature for your e-mail, suppress it.

You will receive confirmation of your subscription from the list server. Following confirmation of your subscription, you can send questions and observations to the other registered participants by addressing e-mail to NDIR grad@mitvma.mit.edu (all registered participants will receive a copy of anything you send to the listserv; you will receive copies of everything other participants send). Should you wish to cancel your subscription, send e-mail to listserv@mitvma.mit.edu with the following text: unsubscribe NDIRgrad (please do not send cancellation requests directly to NDIRgrad because this will inflict them on all other subscribers). If you have any difficulty with your subscription, send notification of your problem to litten@mit.edu.

Jennifer Grant Haworth
Editor

JENNIFER GRANT HAWORTH is assistant professor of higher education at Loyola University Chicago.

The authors note the dearth of cross-disciplinary and cross-institutional studies of student learning outcomes in graduate and professional education and discuss some challenges for those involved in outcomes assessment, including managing the risks of identifying outcomes assessment results.

Challenges in Assessing Outcomes in Graduate and Professional Education

Anne E. Bilder, Clifton F. Conrad

Fueled by calls for more educational accountability from accreditation agencies, industry, legislators, the general public, and students, the past decade has seen the rise of an enduring assessment movement targeted at colleges and universities across the country. Much of the attention has focused on the undergraduate level, but the spotlight increasingly has been placed on graduate and professional education. Diminishing financial resources, an uncertain environment, and public doubts about the capacity of universities to educate professionals for a rapidly changing workplace are all leading to much closer scrutiny of graduate and professional programs.

In response to myriad pressures—including mandates from state governments, accrediting agencies, and institutional governing boards to maintain program quality and preserve limited resources—a number of universities have taken steps to assess their graduate and professional programs. Our own institution, for example, is currently developing an outcomes assessment model for implementation in graduate departments across campus. Anchored in the widely shared assumption that program *outcomes* are perhaps the most important consideration in evaluating and strengthening programs, a growing number of institutions are placing attention on the outcomes of graduate and professional programs, especially outcomes associated with student achievement. The animating intent of this chapter is to help inform such efforts.

Not least because of the highly visible emphasis on undergraduate education for most of the past decade, graduate and professional education has received relatively little attention in the assessment literature. This lacuna may also be accounted for in two other ways. For one, there is the long-held belief that graduate education—and professional education in particular—is in large

NEW DIRECTIONS FOR INSTITUTIONAL RESEARCH, no. 92, Winter 1996 © Jossey-Bass Publishers measure self-regulating through the oversight of professional organizations. For another, unlike undergraduate education, whose generalized nature has lent itself to the type of comprehensive studies such as Ernest Pascarella and Patrick Terenzini's (1991) review of some twenty-six hundred studies of the effects of college on students, scholars have argued that outcomes assessment in graduate and professional education is uniquely tied to individual disciplines and departments (Bowen and Rudenstine, 1992; Kolman, Gallagher, Hossler, and Catania, 1987; Stark, Lowther, and Hagerty, 1986). Hence, there are not compelling reasons for cross-disciplinary studies of graduate and professional program outcomes.

To be sure, a number of field-specific studies have been conducted, such as Hansen's (1990) study of Ph.D.s in economics and Regan-Smith's (1994) study of a graduate teacher education program. Moreover, several institutional studies have been published, including Smart and Hagedorn's (1994) study documenting the relationship between educational strategies and three identified learning outcomes—human relations competency, reflective thinking competency, and research competency—and a study conducted by Kolman and her colleagues (1987) that identifies three broadly defined outcomes of graduate study—career development, values and behaviors, and scholarship—and the influence of graduate school on these outcomes.

Besides these studies, little scholarship has been conducted across disciplines and institutions on the learning outcomes of graduate and professional education. In the area of student learning and development outcomes, Joan Stark and her colleagues (1986) identify eleven generic outcomes of professional education, culled from an extensive review of the field-specific literature. These include six aspects of professional competence—conceptual, technical, contextual, interpersonal, integrative, and adaptive competence—and five attitudinal competencies—career marketability, professional identity, professional ethics, scholarly concern for improvement of the professional, and motivation for continued learning.

A second example of a cross-disciplinary study of learning outcomes at the graduate level is the national study by Conrad, Haworth, and Millar (1993) of master's programs. Based on their interviews with nearly eight hundred students, faculty, administrators, alumni, and employers, the authors report that master's education leads to such positive student outcomes as the development of analytical skills, a "big picture" perspective, the ability to connect theory and practice, and improved communication and professional skills. Finally, in Haworth and Conrad's (1997) book on program quality, the authors draw on their earlier study of forty-seven master's programs in eleven fields of study and identify seventeen attributes of high-quality programs and the positive outcomes that each has on students' learning and development.

In addition to the cross-disciplinary studies of learning outcomes, studies have been conducted in other areas of outcomes of graduate and professional education, particularly in the areas of student retention and time-to-degree (Gillingham, Seneca, and Taussig, 1991; Girves and Wemmerus, 1988; Willie,

Grady, and Hope, 1991). Most notable among these is Bowen and Rudenstine's (1992) comprehensive study of the factors influencing completion rates and time-to-degree among Ph.D. students in the arts and sciences. The authors studied ten prestigious universities and report on the variance of completion rates and time-to-degree among disciplines, departments, and recipients of varying amounts of financial aid, among other variables. Although issues of student retention, job placement, and other outcomes of graduate and professional education are clearly important, our focus throughout will be primarily on student learning and development outcomes.

Overall, while the paucity of literature is disappointing, this gulf may provide the assessment movement a rare opportunity to reflect on the purposes and processes of outcomes assessment. From our perspective, it invites us to identify the most salient challenges associated with assessing the outcomes of graduate and professional programs, not least including the definition of the term "outcome" itself. Further, examination of this concept invites exploration of a little-considered area of outcomes assessment: the consequences of identifying outcomes of graduate and professional programs.

In broad strokes, the purpose of this chapter is to reflect on the outcomes of graduate and professional education in light of one primary question: What are the major challenges facing individuals responsible for conducting outcomes assessment of graduate and professional programs? Because of the absence of much directly relevant literature across fields of study, we draw extensively on our experiences with assessment, along with writings from individuals representing a wide range of fields.

Purposes of Outcomes Assessment

Illuminating the major purposes of assessment is a useful beginning point for discussion of the challenges facing those engaged in outcomes assessment. Such a point of departure is appropriate not only because purposes can animate and serve as useful touchstones for inquiry but also because they can provide solace to researchers that their efforts are at least worthy, if not spiritually uplifting.

At least two major purposes should inform outcomes assessment in graduate and professional education. The first is so obvious that it requires little elaboration: to identify and evaluate quality programs with the intent of maintaining and enhancing quality. Suffice it to say that the assessment literature consistently stresses this purpose through its ubiquitous emphasis on program and institutional quality. For example, Jennifer Grant Haworth and Clifton F. Conrad, in *Emblems of Quality in Higher Education: Developing and Sustaining High-Quality Programs* (1997), provide a template for assessing programs that offers criteria and indicators for evaluating program quality.[1]

There is a second, more implicit, purpose that should guide outcomes assessment in graduate and professional education: to justify the continued existence of programs, if warranted, that have been placed under the assessment microscope. Despite its firmly entrenched position in society, there is widespread skepticism about the value of higher education, including education at the graduate level. For example, Randall Collins argues compellingly in *The Credential Society* (1979) that a college or university diploma is a hollow credential that reflects a lack of coherence between the curriculum and the labor market for which higher education is ostensibly preparing its students.[2] With respect to student development, Leonard L. Baird (1990) has offered a critique of the manner in which graduate and professional programs treat their students. Many other critics both from within and outside the academy have similarly questioned the value of graduate as well as undergraduate education (Anderson, 1992; Douglas, 1992; Smith, 1990; Sykes, 1988). In light of widespread disillusionment with higher education, assessment of the outcomes of graduate and professional education could go a long way in rehabilitating the tarnished images of many postsecondary institutions.

Individuals involved in assessment should decide whether the two reasons discussed above reflect the underlying purposes of assessment and whether there are other equally, or more compelling, reasons. Given the extent to which purposes are likely to influence the selection of methods and approaches to outcomes assessment, this threshold issue merits serious consideration.

Who Designs and Executes the Assessment?

The challenge of deciding who should be responsible for assessment is a critical one, because issues of power and expertise invariably intersect. With respect to power, it is readily understood that whoever enjoys formal authority is more or less in a position to advance any personal agendas. To be sure, a potential problem with conceptualizing the challenge this way is that it can lead to an either-or situation in which one individual—or group of individuals—is privileged over others. Still, we believe that the potential value of asking this question is considerable: it invites us to consider a multiplicity of interests whose voices merit a hearing. There may be roles for many actors in the design and implementation of an outcomes assessment of graduate and professional education.

For obvious reasons, faculty and administrators should be viewed as major voices in outcomes assessment at the graduate and professional levels. Students, too, can help design outcomes assessment, since they represent a formal link between education and the labor market and thus can bring valuable perspectives to assessment. Accreditation agencies also warrant consideration as a voice in designing and implementing a program of outcomes assessment. In recent years, many of these entities—specialized as well as regional accrediting bodies—have been involved in reform in graduate and professional education, and they are usually attuned to the interests of industry as well as the larger society. Representatives from state higher education agencies, particularly since they hold the purse strings for public institutions, may merit inclusion. Likewise, representatives of industry and professional associations may be appropriate participants, since preparation in many graduate and professional programs is aimed at helping students enhance their workplace contributions. Finally, scholars and institutional researchers can contribute valuable perspectives to help inform the design and implementation of assessment initiatives. Whether all or only some of these stakeholders are heard in outcomes assessment efforts, considering their voices reminds us of the broader university community and returns us to the purposes of assessment.

Challenges in Identifying Outcomes

A third challenge is: What constitutes an "outcome" for the purpose of assessment of graduate and professional education? Closely related is the issue of the means by which faculty and others identify those outcomes. We do not intend here to develop an exhaustive list of outcomes. As noted above, the literature provides few studies of outcomes across fields, suggesting implicitly as well as explicitly that many outcomes are uniquely associated with specific programs and institutions (Bowen and Rudenstine, 1992; Kolman, Gallagher, Hossler, and Catania, 1987; Stark, Lowther, and Hagerty, 1986), as well as with individual stakeholders. Moreover, such a list would have to acknowledge the multiplicity of types of outcomes, including student learning and development outcomes, student retention and placement outcomes, and societal outcomes, among others. Instead, we prefer to focus on major challenges surrounding the identification of student learning and development outcomes and, in so doing, hope that those responsible for outcomes assessment may enhance their appreciation for the complexity of the task and proceed with both greater caution and the greater confidence that comes from knowing in advance about some of the hazards.

By now, the term "outcome" is probably too firmly entrenched in the language of assessment to be easily dislodged. And yet many are uncomfortable with the word in the context of education. For some, the word represents an inappropriate adoption of business rhetoric—inappropriate not least because we remain skeptical that education can be reduced to commercial metaphors. Despite varying amounts of discomfort with the word, however, we continue to use it, because most of us firmly believe that "something happens" as a result of education, and this concept can help to describe what that something is. Moreover, many of us share the belief that while there are qualities that make education uniquely ill-suited to the meticulous dissection often used in assessment in industry, education should not be beyond accountability.

Ironically, rather than obscuring the nature of graduate and professional education, using the term "outcomes" may actually help establish its salience and uniqueness, because the ambiguities and complexities associated with the word underscore, in turn, the ambiguities and complexities of graduate and professional study. In explicating outcomes, we are compelled to search for answers to questions about graduate and professional education and the role of the university in society.

One of the major ambiguities encountered with the use of the word "outcome" is that it often is used synonymously with the term "benefit." Thus, virtually the only outcomes identified are "good" outcomes: potential negative outcomes are ignored or overlooked. For example, in their work on the outcomes of professional education, Joan Stark and her colleagues (1986) relied on the literature to identify eleven "generic" outcomes. Not one of the eleven outcomes expresses a negative consequence of professional education. Several reasons may account for this. For one, the literature reviewed by Stark and her associates itself may have equated "outcome" with "benefit." For another, the original studies themselves may well not have found any significant negative outcomes of professional education. For still another, Stark and the authors of the original studies may not have consistently distinguished between actual and desired outcomes. To the extent that the studies reflect desired outcomes, any negative outcomes naturally would have been omitted. Any or all of these problems might account for the absence of negative outcomes and the tendency to conflate outcomes with benefits.

Among the few studies that even mention the negative outcomes of graduate education is Martha Regan-Smith's research on the outcomes that teachers experience, or anticipate experiencing, in graduate school. Regan-Smith found that the teacher-subjects in her study most often mentioned the fear of the "burden of presumed competence" as an important outcome of graduate education; that is, "Having attended a graduate school with a considerable reputation [Harvard], the teachers and administrators feared that others would assume that they were more competent than they were" (1994, p. 55). Likewise, some economists have argued that a cost-benefit analysis of graduate education reveals that the costs to students may significantly exceed the benefits. These economists have based their findings on calculations of opportunity cost, finding that students have foregone the opportunity to earn significant salaries out of school while—at the same time—they are paying substantial fees to stay in graduate school with no guarantee of future employment. According to Harrison Shull: "It is certainly true that the major bearer of the cost of higher education is the student, and we ought to keep that firmly in mind. . . . As far as I am concerned, the economic returns of higher education beyond the bachelor's degree are probably close to zero and in some cases actually negative" (1982, p. 14). Similar sentiments have been reflected in studies examining the time-to-degree of doctoral students (Gillingham, Seneca, and Taussig, 1991, p. 449).

While opening up the concept of "outcomes" at the graduate and professional level to potential negative consequences can have its downside, we believe it is worth doing nonetheless. For conversely, failing to acknowledge negative outcomes can obscure problems and seriously undermine efforts to improve program quality at the graduate and professional level. In addition, acknowledging negative outcomes can help preempt those critics who would justifiably argue that any analysis failing to identify problems can only be judged superficial. From our perspective, a key task for those involved in outcomes assessment is to ensure that both "good" and "bad" outcomes of graduate and professional education are given due consideration.

A second complexity in identifying outcomes is the problem of causation. Our personal interest in law reminds us of the appropriateness of the analogy of the legal preoccupation with the issue of causation. In the area of negligence, for example, proximate cause—that is, whether the action or inaction of the defendant directly caused the injury at issue in the lawsuit—is a critical element in the plaintiff's case. While a lower standard of causation—such as indirect causation—may be accepted in education, we remain committed to the notion that for something to be considered an outcome, there must be some connection between the graduate or professional program and that outcome. This is an even stickier problem for education than for law, because educators and scholars often do not fully understand relationships between teaching, learning, and student outcomes. Thus, attributing cause-and-effect in these programs is at best uncertain, especially because graduate and professional programs represent such advanced levels of education. It is difficult to link specific competencies, knowledge, or other considerations to specific features of the graduate or professional school curriculum and environment.

Smart and Hagedorn (1994), however, have attempted to document such a relationship. In their study of doctoral students at a single university, they found that students' perceptions of their development in human relations, reflective thinking, and research competency were related to the types of educational strategies they perceive their doctoral programs as employing. While instructive, the study clearly needs to be replicated elsewhere to further document and confirm the existence of such a relationship in other institutions.

Last and not least, in light of the trend to recognize learning as a lifelong activity the question naturally arises: At what point do we measure outcomes? Should we be concerned with both short-term and long-term outcomes? In the rush to provide results in response to external calls for accountability, the long-term outcomes of graduate and professional education may be detrimentally neglected. Few scholars have explored the challenge of deciding when to identify outcomes. Although Regan-Smith (1994, p. 56) posed this question to her graduate students, "When will you best appreciate the benefit of your graduate school experience?," the participants felt that the full effects of their graduate school experience could not be determined while they were still in school. While they anticipated that appreciation of those benefits would come with their return to teaching, the speculative nature of their response rendered the question essentially unanswered.

Arguably, this question may be implied in scholarly writing that posits that there are social benefits of graduate and professional education. The willingness of scholars such as Derek Bok (1982) and Clark Kerr (1995) to look beyond individual benefits to societal benefits implies an appreciation for the value of long-term outcomes, since we would presume that the time frame for graduate and professional education to make a measurable impact on society is much longer than at the undergraduate level. Nevertheless, this notion is never made explicit. From our perspective, a major challenge for individuals responsible for outcomes assessment is to weigh the considerations involved in using short-term and long-term outcomes for assessment purposes.

Wise Usage: Managing the Risks of Outcomes Assessment Results

One other formidable challenge remains: ensuring the wise use of outcomes assessment results. As a beginning point, wise use can mean an effort to apply results to stated goals, such as to justify, as well as improve, the quality of graduate and professional programs. More broadly, we believe that wise use should also recognize the inherent risks to institutions in implementing outcomes assessment results, such as the threat that outcomes assessment may pose to such cherished institutional traditions as academic freedom.

From our perspective, the challenge for those responsible for outcomes assessment is to carefully manage the risks of outcomes assessment results to ensure their wise use consistent with the goals of assessment and the purposes of the college or university. In some cases, this will require finding a way to reconcile the need for improvement and accountability with institutional integrity and autonomy. In other cases, it might invite a reexamination of academic traditions. In any event, the results of outcomes assessment should help illuminate those salient characteristics of the university that emerge through the strict scrutiny of assessment and, in so doing, provide insight into ways to strengthen graduate and professional education.

To begin, one of the primary risks in implementing outcomes assessment results in graduate and professional education is the potential threat to institutional autonomy. This may manifest itself in at least two closely related ways: the erosion of the protections afforded by academic freedom and the weakening of the traditional barrier between the university and the courts. As to the first, the concept of academic freedom represents a defining characteristic of the modern American college and university (Bok, 1982; Gross, 1968; Hofstadter and Metzger, 1955). In brief, academic freedom protects, at the very least, the professor's right to teach and pursue research according to the dictates of his or her own mind, unrestricted by external and institutional interference. It is a right upheld by the U.S. Supreme Court, which carved out a place for academic freedom in the United States Constitution as an extension of the First Amendment (*Sweezy* v *New Hampshire,* 1957; *Keyishian* v *Board of Regents,* 1967), and one embraced by contemporary historians and legal scholars (Hook, 1969; Metzger, 1988; Olivas, 1993). Recently, the concept of academic freedom has been, if not explicitly, at least implicitly extended both to institutions themselves and their students through several federal court decisions. In so doing, these courts have suggested that there may be a correlate to professorial academic freedom for the institution and its students.

A very significant problem arises in outcomes assessment when the results lead to mandated reforms—in faculty pedagogy, for example—that infringe upon academic freedom. Putting aside the issue of legal claims that might arise out of such circumstances, the more important concern is that the erosion of such a cherished tradition would significantly alter the essential character of the university as a place that embraces above all else the "freedom to inquire" or, to put it another way, the metaphor of the "marketplace of ideas." To the extent that assessment results lead to the mandated implementation of alternative approaches to teaching and learning, faculty—and students'—former freedoms may be diminished. Experimentation, creativity, and serendipity—all valued under the auspices of academic freedom—may likewise be reduced. Given the centrality of academic freedom to the contemporary university, we suggest that those responsible for outcomes assessment consciously seek to reconcile academic freedom with assessment results. Otherwise, the university—including graduate and professional education—may well be reconstituted in a way that diminishes academic freedom.

Closely related to the risk of the erosion of academic freedom is the danger that outcomes assessment results may expose colleges and universities to stricter judicial scrutiny. For several decades, there has existed a judicially created boundary between the university and the courts in academic matters.[3] This continues to be the prevailing jurisprudence, even in cases that directly relate to the concerns of outcomes assessment: educational malpractice.[4] While no court has recognized the claim against an institution based on the quality of its graduate or professional programs, to the extent that outcomes assessment results begin to identify something approaching standards of quality for graduate and professional education, the courts may no longer be able to rely upon the lack of standards by which to measure quality as a reason to defer to educational institutions. In turn, the barrier between the university and the courts will be weakened, and the university will be at risk to additional judicial scrutiny that may further limit its autonomy.

For those involved in outcomes assessment, the challenge is to appreciate the risks involved in establishing identifiable criteria and indicators in assessing outcomes, as well as risks in determining the overall impact that any resulting judicial involvement might have on quality in graduate and professional education. Managing such risks may result in an acceptance, for example, that any judicial interference may in fact further promote quality education by exposing weaknesses in the present curriculum.

Still another risk in implementing outcomes assessment results is the danger that the preoccupation with outcomes may inevitably lead to greater concern about inputs, resulting in further restricting opportunities for students to be accepted into graduate and professional programs. As we were completing this piece, the United States Court of Appeals for the Fifth Circuit published its opinion in *Hopwood* v *Texas* (No. 94–50569, March 18, 1996) in which it overruled the District Court's opinion upholding the use of race and ethnicity as criteria in admissions decisions.[5] This decision did not come down in a vacuum; rather, it is consistent with the current context of a heightened awareness of issues of access to universities and questions about what constitutes merit. In light of the present political climate, those who are concerned with placing further restrictions on access to educational opportunities should be wary of the potential consequences of implementing the results of outcomes assessment. Findings that identify specific desired outcomes of graduate and professional education, for example, may cause university administrators to tailor admissions criteria to better approximate an "ideal type" of student who may more readily be able to achieve those outcomes. The narrowing of admissions standards, especially as coupled with stricter notions of what constitutes "merit," may preclude many minorities and other disadvantaged individuals from obtaining graduate and professional training.

Individuals responsible for outcomes assessment in graduate and professional education, we believe, should at the least seek to balance concerns for accountability with concerns about access and equal opportunity. More idealistically, it is our hope that the design and results of outcomes assessment might provide an opportunity for institutions to reinvent a concept of the idea of merit that recognizes the potential of diverse students for enhancing the quality of universities.

Conclusion

In many ways, for both assessment advocates and those responsible for designing and implementing assessment plans, this chapter may be, on the one hand, too critical, and on the other, merely raise more questions than it has answered. We, however, are not discouraged. For us, highlighting some of the major challenges of assessment merely serves to persuade us further of the value in assessment and, correspondingly, the need to approach it carefully and cautiously. In the end, we believe that a major value of outcomes assessment ultimately may rest in the process itself, rather than in the end product—the "outcomes"—of outcomes assessment. For in identifying outcomes and deciding how to reconcile them with (or reinvent) institutional traditions, such activity refocuses these issues on the critical questions of the purposes of graduate and professional education and the role of the university in society. Through focusing on challenges involved in the outcomes assessment process, we invite others to join with us in a continuing conversation that, over time, may help ensure that outcomes assessment enriches rather than diminishes our colleges and universities.

Notes

1. This template is anchored in the idea that high-quality programs are those in which students, faculty, and administrators invest significant time and effort in mutually supportive teaching and learning.

2. See, for example, *Martin* v *Parish,* 805 F.2d 583 (5th Cir. 1986), *Parate* v *Isibor,* 868 F.2d 821 (6th Cir. 1989), and *Bishop* v *Oronov,* 926 F.2d 1066 (11th Cir. 1991).

3. In such cases as *University of Missouri* v *Horowitz,* 435 U.S. 78 (1978) and *Regents of the University of Michigan* v *Ewing,* 474 U.S. 214 (1985), the U.S. Supreme Court articulated reasons why such a barrier should exist.

4. Educational malpractice raises similar issues about quality of education, as does the assessment movement. To date, however, few courts have been willing to recognize a theory of educational malpractice. Among the reasons courts cite for denying claims based on educational malpractice are the lack of an identifiable standard for measuring what constitutes "good teaching" or a "good education," concern about judicial interference in the daily administrations of colleges and universities, problems of causation, and fear of excessive litigation. Notably, only the court in *Andre* v *Pace University,* 618 N.Y.S. 2d 975 (1994) has accepted this theory, and this case can be easily distinguished, based on the special facts of the case and unique circumstances.

5. The Fifth Circuit Court purported to overrule the Supreme Court's decision in *Bakke* v *Regents of the University of California,* 438 U.S. 265 (1978), holding that race can no longer be used as a criterion in admissions decisions, even under the justifications of diversity.

ANNE E. BILDER is an attorney and is currently pursuing a doctoral degree in educational administration at the University of Wisconsin-Madison.

CLIFTON F. CONRAD is professor of higher education at the University of Wisconsin-Madison.

New demographics have far-reaching implications both for the demand
for advanced-degree programs and for their delivery and evaluation.

Assessing Demand for Graduate and Professional Programs

Peter D. Syverson

Over the past two decades, the graduate education enterprise in the United States has experienced profound change in both the numbers and demographic composition of the graduate student population. Two changes, in particular, stand out. First, student and employer demand for graduate education greatly intensified during this period. Developments in the U.S. economy spurred unprecedented changes in the workplace, elevating the need for more highly skilled, knowledgeable, professional workers. Second, dramatic changes occurred in the graduate student population. In contrast to the 1970s, the typical graduate student today is no longer a recent undergraduate pursuing full-time study but an older, working professional studying part-time. Not surprisingly, these changes have influenced the content, structure, and delivery of graduate education as we know it today.

In this chapter, I elaborate on these changes and assess what they potentially mean for consumer demand for graduate education. In so doing, I divide the chapter into four sections. The first provides historical background on trends in graduate enrollment and degrees over the last two decades and describes the forces shaping those trends. The second section describes the current status of students in graduate school and develops a demographic portrait of them, drawing on a variety of data from the Council of Graduate Schools/Graduate Record Examination (CGS/GRE) Survey of Graduate Enrollment, the Institute of International Education (IIE) Open Doors survey, and the National Center for Education Statistics (NCES) National Postsecondary Student Aid Study (NPSAS). The third section explores anticipated future trends in graduate education in light of student aspirations, as well as the current and future job market situation for advanced-degree recipients. Finally, in the fourth section, I discuss how institutional researchers can monitor the national and regional changes in demand for graduate education and assess student demand for a particular institution and its programs.

Two Decades of Change

The past twenty years have produced great economic and political change in the United States, with the end of the Cold War, the emergence of new, highly competitive economies in the Pacific Rim, and the transition of the United States from an industrial to a knowledge-based economy. During this time, the U.S. graduate enterprise experienced shifts in the number of students enrolled in graduate and first-professional programs,[1] the demographic composition of those students, and student demand for graduate degrees in different fields of study.

Graduate Enrollment. Two periods define the changes in graduate enrollment in the two decades from 1974 to the present: one of relative stability between 1974 and 1984 and one of growth between 1984 and the present. Graduate enrollment grew quickly from 1974 to 1976, but then leveled off and remained at about 1.3 million from 1976 to 1984. During that time, overall graduate enrollment grew at a rate of just 1 percent a year, mostly accounted for by the 1974 to 1976 increase. Beginning in 1985, however, graduate enrollment increased rapidly, rising from 1.4 million students in 1984 to 1.7 million in 1994, an overall increase of 25 percent and an annual rate of 2 percent (National Center for Education Statistics, 1996).

Three forces were instrumental in the shift from the stability of the 1976–1984 period to the growth that followed: the downturn in hiring in the early 1980s, the upgrading of job requirements, and the movement of women into the professional labor force. Bachelor's degree recipients in the early 1980s faced a very difficult job market (Lindquist, 1983) and, as a result, many entered graduate programs, primarily at the master's degree level, with the expectation that job prospects would be better with a master's degree and that the job market would improve by the time of graduation. In addition, a variety of professions, such as education and health sciences, began to require higher degree requirements for entry or promotion. Finally, women who took time out from careers following the bachelor's degree entered graduate programs to earn up-to-date credentials in order to re-enter the labor force.

Underlying these patterns of stability and growth were substantial changes in both the diversity of the graduate student population and the fields in which students pursued graduate study. One of the more important of these trends has been the increasing participation of women in graduate programs.[2] Between 1974 and 1994, the number of women pursuing graduate study grew steadily. Interestingly, this occurred despite the relative stability of graduate enrollments throughout the 1970s. In fact, the number of women graduate students has grown at a consistent 2 to 3 percent annual rate over the last twenty years. Comparison of the end points of this two-decade trend show the dramatic upsurge in women's participation in graduate education: in 1974, women constituted 44 percent of graduate enrollment; by 1994, their representation had increased to 55 percent. Overall, the number of women enrolled in grad-uate programs jumped 80 percent between 1974 and 1994, while the number of men increased just 17 percent.

The number of U.S. minority-group members enrolled in graduate pro-grams also increased between 1976 and 1994.[3] During this period, the num-ber of Asian and Hispanic graduate students more than doubled, with Asian enrollment rising from 25,000 to 73,000 and Hispanic enrollment from 26,000 to 64,000. African American graduate enrollment followed a different path, decreasing 15 percent during the first eight years of this period, then increas-ing consistently from 1984 to 1994. Over the entire period, the number of African Americans enrolled in graduate programs increased from 79,000 in 1976 to 111,000 in 1994.[4] In the last two decades, the number of American Indians pursuing graduate degrees increased as well, from about 5,000 in 1976 to 8,000 in 1994.

Coincident with the impressive increases in the enrollment of women and minority-group members, an unprecedented number of international students entered U.S. graduate schools between 1974 and 1994. According to the NCES (1996), the number of nonresident aliens enrolled in graduate programs rose steeply from 72,000 in 1976 to 180,000 in 1994. An influx of students from the Pacific Rim accounted for most of this growth. In 1995, four of the five leading countries of origin for international students were Pacific Rim nations (Syverson, 1996). In recent years, however, the number of international stu-dents has decreased from a peak of 184,000 in 1992 to 180,000 in 1994. According to the IIE (Davis, 1995), students from Pacific Rim countries are finding more opportunities for graduate study at home, as their countries begin to invest more heavily in their higher education and research infrastructures.

First-Professional Enrollment. Over the past two decades, enrollment in first-professional programs has followed quite a different path than that of grad-uate school enrollment. While most of the increase in graduate enrollment occurred during the past ten years, the strongest growth in first-professional enrollment occurred in the first decade, rising from 235,452 in 1974 to 278,598 in 1984, an average increase of just under 2 percent per year. After 1984, how-ever, first-professional enrollment declined to 267,109 in 1988, 4 percent lower than 1984. This downward trend has since reversed, with first-professional enrollment moving steadily up to 294,713 in 1994 (National Center for Edu-cation Statistics, 1996).

As with gradate education, women have entered first-professional programs in rapidly increasing numbers. The enrollment of women in first-professional programs has tripled, growing from 41,373 in 1974 to 120,757 in 1994, an average increase of almost 6 percent per year. During this twenty-year period, women's participation in first-professional programs grew from 18 percent of first-professional enrollment in 1974 to 41 percent in 1994 (National Center for Education Statistics, 1996).

U.S. minority-group enrollment also increased in first-professional degree programs over the past two decades. The enrollment of Asian Americans grew at the fastest pace, rising from about 4,100 in 1976 to 27,600 in 1994, a six-fold increase. Meanwhile, the number of Hispanics enrolled in first-professional programs tripled (4,500 to 13,400), while the number of blacks nearly doubled (from 11,200 to 20,700). The growth among black U.S. citizens and permanent residents was seen largely among women, paralleling the trends in graduate enrollment. American Indian enrollment remained relatively steady, although there have been increases in recent years (National Center for Education Statistics, 1996).

Student demand for law and medical programs—the two largest fields in first-professional study—followed somewhat different paths over the 1974 to 1994 period. According to the American Bar Association (1995), enrollment in law schools grew during the 1970s and early 1980s but declined until 1987. Since then, law enrollment increased to 134,784 in 1994, an average of 1.2 percent per year. Again, women's participation fueled much of this increase, growing rapidly over the two decades and, in 1994, accounting for 43 percent of total law school enrollment. Medical school enrollment also decreased in the mid-1980s, following a peak of 67,327 in 1983. However, unlike law, the subsequent increases have not surpassed the 1983 peak. As in other graduate fields, the enrollment of women in medicine has grown steadily in the past two decades, increasing from 7,828 in 1974 to 26,854 in 1994. Women now account for 40 percent of the nation's medical students (Jolly and Hudley, 1995).

Graduate Degrees. Given the time lag between enrollment and receipt of degree, we should expect to see many of the same trends described above reflected in degree statistics. This is especially the case for master's degrees, where time-to-degree is short and completion rates are relatively high. At the doctoral level, the relationship between enrollment and degrees is less direct because of considerably longer time-to-degree ratios (Simmons and Thurgood, 1995) and completion (Bowen and Rudenstine, 1992).

Master's Degrees. As expected, the two distinct periods of graduate enrollment mentioned earlier are reflected in the data on master's degrees. As graduate enrollment leveled off in the mid-to-late 1970s, so did the number of master's degrees granted by U.S. institutions. And as graduate enrollment entered the growth phase of the mid-1980s, so grew the number of master's degrees granted. Indeed, since 1984, the number of master's degrees conferred increased by 30 percent, from 284,263 to 387,070 (National Center for Education Statistics, 1996). This upswing is attributable to the same factors cited earlier for graduate enrollment increases, especially employer demand for more highly skilled and knowledgeable workers and changes in entry-level and promotion requirements in some professions (such as physical therapy and social work) (Conrad, Haworth, and Millar, 1993).

Over the past twenty years, there have been discernable shifts in demand for master's degrees across fields of study. Four broad fields followed the general pattern of moderate increases—the physical sciences, engineering, life sciences, and public administration. Two fields—social sciences and humanities—experienced a pattern of degree decreases in the first decade of the period, followed by increases in the second decade.

Arguably the most dramatic shifts have occurred in the fields of education and business, the two largest fields for master's degree recipients. Master's degrees in education increased 11 percent from 1974 to 1977, but then plummeted 41 percent from 1977 to 1985. The numbers had recovered somewhat by 1994 but were still 12 percent below the 1974 figure. In contrast, the number of master's degrees in business grew rapidly over the entire period, rising at an average annual rate of 5 percent. In 1974, education accounted for 41 percent of all master's degrees conferred and business, some 12 percent. By 1994, a notable shift in demand had transpired with education and business awarding 26 percent and 24 percent of all master's degrees, respectively.

Doctoral Degrees. Paralleling the trends in graduate enrollment and master's degrees granted, the two decades 1974–1984 and 1984–1994 represent distinct time periods for doctoral degrees granted. During the former, the number of doctoral degrees conferred declined slightly, from approximately 34,000 degrees in 1974 to 33,000 in 1984. Thereafter, the number of doctoral degrees awarded by U.S. colleges and universities began a steady climb, rising from 33,653 in 1985 to more than 40,000 degrees in 1994 (National Center for Education Statistics, 1996).

In terms of shifts in demand across fields of study, nearly all major fields experienced a decrease in the number of doctorates granted from 1974 to 1984. This decrease was especially pronounced in the humanities, where the number of doctorates dropped 51 percent from 5,170 in 1974 to a low of 3,429 in 1985. Since the mid-1980s, the number of doctorates earned in most fields has increased. The exception is in education, where the number of new doctorates decreased from 1974 to 1984 and has remained below the 1970s peak. In fact, education and the humanities are the only two major fields in which current doctoral awards are below 1974 levels (National Research Council, 1996). This is an indication that graduate education is in an era of segmented markets, where economic and demographic trends have differential impact on demand for various degree levels, programs, and fields.

First-Professional Degrees. While the number of graduate degrees declined in the late 1970s and early 1980s, first-professional degrees saw their strongest growth during that time, increasing from 53,816 in 1974 to 74,468 in 1984. Following a peak in 1985, first-professional degrees decreased through 1988, then increased through 1994 (National Center for Education Statistics, 1996).

Paralleling trends in law school enrollment, the number of law degrees conferred reached a high in the mid-1980s (37,491 in 1985) then oscillated between 35,000 and 36,000 until 1990. Following rapid increases in law enrollment, which began in the late 1980s, the number of law degrees conferred rose steeply beginning in 1990. As with law enrollment, the number of law degrees earned by women has increased substantially over the past two decades, now at 17,122, almost four times the number in 1974. Over 37 percent of law degrees are now earned by women (National Center for Education Statistics, 1996).

Medical degrees conferred over this period grew from 11,356 in 1974 to an all-time high of 16,041 in 1985 but then dropped to just over 15,000 in

1991, and have since hovered in the low 15,000s. Despite the inconsistent overall trend, the number of women earning medical degrees increased rapidly over the last two decades, more than tripling from 1974 to 1994. Meanwhile, the 1994 total of 9,544 men earning medical degrees is at its lowest over the entire twenty-year period (National Center for Education Statistics, 1996).

Present Status and the New Demographics of Graduate Education

Following the sustained growth in the last decade, graduate education is moving into a third phase, that of market segmentation. In the current era, demand for graduate education is characterized by growth in some areas but decline in others. This differentiation of the market is evident in the most recent trends in graduate applications and enrollment.

Recent Application and Enrollment Trends. An examination of recent trends in graduate enrollment and applications provides an indication of current student demand. From an era of overall annual growth rates of 2 percent, with consistent growth across fields, demand has shifted to annual growth rates of 1 percent and increases in some fields but decreases in others. For example, enrollment in health sciences grew at an annual rate of 6 percent, the fastest rate of growth of all major fields. The biological sciences, social sciences, and public administration all grew at between 3 and 4 percent per year. In contrast, after two decades of sustained growth, business enrollments have begun to turn down. Enrollments in engineering and the physical sciences decreased as well, probably as a result of the decline in the number of non-U.S. citizens entering U.S. graduate programs (Syverson and Welch, 1996).

Graduate applications provide an additional indicator of changing student demand for graduate study. In 1994, the institutions surveyed in the CGS/GRE Survey of Graduate Enrollment reported receiving more than one million applications for graduate study. This is an increase of 2 percent from 1993 and continues a trend of increasing interest in graduate study. However, as with enrollment, applications have shifted from growth across all fields to increases in some and decreases in others. For example, from 1990 to 1994, applications increased at a 15 percent annual rate in the health sciences, a 12 percent rate in public administration, and a 7 percent annual rate in the social sciences. On the other hand, from 1993 to 1994, applications were down 2 percent or more in business, education, and engineering. Especially noteworthy are the rapid application increases in the health sciences, public administration, and the social sciences. This development, in particular, suggests that graduate education has moved from an era of uniform growth to a segmented market, where student demand is growing for some fields but declining for others.

Changing Demographics. A second influence on demand for graduate education is the changing demographic picture. According the Bureau of the Census (Day, 1996), the 25–39-year-old cohort, which encompasses about 70 percent of graduate students, will decrease by 11 percent between 1995 and 2005. More importantly, this population will become considerably more diverse. Over the next twenty years, substantial growth will occur in the 25–39-year-old minority population, led by rapid increases in the number of Asian and Hispanic Americans. At the same time, the number of white U.S. residents will decline by 22 percent. By 2015, minorities will make up 37 percent of this age cohort, up from the 1995 figure of 28 percent.

Note, however, that the relationship between demographics and future graduate enrollment is likely to be indirect, because graduate enrollment is such a small percentage of the overall population. The 1.7 million graduate students in 1994, for example, were about 3 percent of the 25–39-year-old cohort. Nevertheless, demographic changes will inevitably influence both the population from which graduate students are drawn and the population that will be served by recipients of graduate degrees.

The New American Graduate Student. Taken together, the influences described above—market segmentation, changing demographics, and changing demand from employers for individuals with advanced degrees—have contributed to a profound change in the graduate student population. Although writing about master's degree students, much of what Borchert (1994) notes is also true at the doctoral level: "The traditional view of a master's student as a white male attending graduate school full time immediately after finishing the baccalaureate degree is no longer valid. The typical master's degree student in the 1990s attends school part-time, is older, probably has worked after obtaining the baccalaureate, and is most likely to be female" (p. 11).

New statistical data from the National Postsecondary Student Aid Study (NPSAS) support Borchert's contention. Two-thirds of all master's degree students, and nearly one-half of all doctoral students, attend school on a part-time basis. Women make up more than 50 percent of master's students and 38 percent of doctoral students. Moreover, the average age of graduate students stands at thirty-three, with about one-fifth of students over the age of forty. More than one-half are married, and many have dependents. And nearly 90 percent of master's students and 75 percent of doctoral students work more than thirty hours per week, earning an average of more than $30,000 per year (National Center for Education Statistics, 1993a).

These statistics are indicative of a population of adults returning to school on a part-time basis while employed full-time. The new American graduate student is not just an older undergraduate, but an adult with a career, family, dependents, and debt.[5] These developments have important implications for the type of degree programs and fields of study that will appeal to and meet the needs of adult students, as well as the delivery systems used for those programs. Beyond that, there are implications for how adult students will evaluate the utility and quality of graduate programs and, in turn, how institutions should assess those programs.

Future Prospects: The Uneasy Future

While we cannot predict the future with any certainty, we can consider the broad factors that are likely to influence the future demand for graduate education.

This section begins with a discussion of student expectations, and then proceeds to explore the other major influences on demand—job requirements, international student mobility, increasing student diversity, and student perceptions of the current job market for recipients of advanced degrees.

Student Expectations. Two recent surveys conducted by the NCES queried students about their educational expectations, asking them to indicate the highest degree they planned to earn. The first survey, conducted in 1991, asked recent baccalaureate recipients (1989–90) about their educational aspirations (National Center for Education Statistics, 1993b). Most planned to pursue some sort of postbaccalaureate education, with 62 percent aspiring to earn a master's degree, 13 percent a doctoral degree, and 8 percent a first-professional degree.

A similar question was asked of respondents to the 1992–93 NPSAS survey. The survey results revealed that for bachelor's degree students in 1993, 53 percent expected to have the master's as their highest degree, 20 percent planned to earn a doctoral degree, and 6 percent a first-professional degree (National Center for Education Statistics, 1993a). A survey of college freshman (Sax, Astin, Korn, and Mahoney, 1995) yielded slightly different results, with 37 percent planning to earn a master's degree, 14 percent a doctoral degree, and 12 percent a medical or law degree.

Labor Market Demand. Over the past ten years, much of the growth in graduate education—particularly at the master's level—has been in degree programs typically categorized as professional. This is particularly evident in the fields of business, health sciences, engineering, and public administration. Rapid changes in knowledge and technology have significantly increased employer demand for advanced professional development, and that demand is reflected in recent enrollment increases. The "tremendous growth in the number of master's degrees awarded can be traced to the need for continued professional development" (O'Brien, 1992). In 1994, for example, roughly 84 percent of master's degrees were granted in professional fields, with 16 percent granted in liberal arts and science fields (National Center for Education Statistics, 1996). This demand from employers has an influence on doctoral study as well, especially considering the current tight job market experienced by many new Ph.D.'s.

Another influence on the demand for graduate study is the upgrading of credentials for advancement in professions. This is especially common in health and social science fields such as physical therapy and social work. For example, one can practice as a physical therapist with a bachelor's degree, but the master's degree is recommended for those seeking to teach, conduct research, or gain promotion to an administrative position (Bureau of Labor Statistics, 1996).

International Students. International students have been an increasingly important component of graduate education for the past two decades. While they make up just 11 percent of total graduate enrollment, they are much more influential at the doctoral level, where temporary-visa holders earned 28 percent of doctorates in science and engineering in 1994 (National Research Council, 1996).

As noted earlier, the number of international students rose rapidly from 1974 to 1992 but decreased thereafter. Perhaps the most dramatic change in international student flow occurred as the result of an abrupt downturn in the number of students coming to the United States from major Asian countries (Davis, 1995). Because Asian countries account for more than two-thirds of international graduate enrollment, this change had a substantial impact on overall U.S. graduate enrollment. From 1994 to 1995, for example, the number of graduate students from China and Taiwan decreased 10 percent; Indian graduate student enrollments in the United States dipped some 4 percent. A 15 percent increase in the number of students from Eastern Europe (particularly Russia and the former U.S.S.R.) helped to offset these decreases.

A major factor behind this change in student flow is the substantial investment Asian countries have made in their research and development and higher education systems (National Science Foundation, 1993). This investment has increased educational opportunities at home, making it possible for students to remain in their homes or neighboring counties for graduate study. As a result, "for many students a U.S. graduate education may become less attractive than home-grown opportunities" (Davis, 1995). While many of the best students will continue to come to the United States, the supply of international students will be much less dependable than in the past, and institutions will have to compete harder for high-quality students.

Diversity in the Graduate Student Population. As previously mentioned, the increasing participation of women and U.S. minority-group members has accounted for much of the recent growth in graduate enrollment. That trend is likely to continue, particularly considering the labor market demands for graduate-level education for entry and promotion. However, much like the situation with international students, institutions should not expect that the high growth rates will be sustained indefinitely. It may be, for example, that we will begin to see an attenuation in the growth rate of women enrolling in graduate education, now that women account for more than one-half of all graduate degrees.

Perceptions of the Job Market. Nearly as influential as employer demand is a student's perception of the career potential of a given course of study. In recent years, there has been a lively debate about job market prospects for new Ph.D.'s in science and engineering. Data from the National Science Foundation indicate that the overall unemployment rate for scientists and engineers with doctorates in 1993 was 1.6 percent, which is considerably below the national unemployment rate (Wilkinson, 1995).

There is evidence, however, that recent Ph.D. recipients are having trouble securing permanent positions. Employment plans data from the NRC's Survey of Earned Doctorates show that the percentage of new Ph.D. recipients still seeking a position at the time the doctorate was conferred has risen in recent years (National Research Council, 1996). In addition, reports from science and engineering disciplinary societies indicate unemployment rates in the summer and fall following 1993 graduation were as high as 17 percent (Gaddy, 1995). Of course, new Ph.D.'s eventually find employment, and these initial high unemployment rates drop sharply in the year following graduation, as new graduates secure positions.

Nevertheless, the perception of a tight job market can influence student demand for graduate study. In their surveys of recent doctoral recipients, the American Institute of Physics found that the percentage of Ph.D.'s with no job offers following graduation rose in the early 1990s, peaking at 15 percent in 1995 (Neuschatz and Mulvey, 1995; Dodge and Mulvey, 1996). This job market stress has affected the decision of potential students to pursue graduate study in physics. From 1992 to 1995, for instance, the number of first-year graduate students in physics decreased a total of 21 percent from 1992 to 1995 (Mulvey and Dodge, 1996).

New Delivery Systems. Distance learning technologies are also likely to influence student demand for graduate education. The new knowledge-based economy will require workers to upgrade continuously their professional-level skills, thereby likely increasing demand for both traditional graduate degrees and shorter-term credential programs. In addition, as the United States enters an era when job mobility is commonplace, institutions will be expected to provide graduate education through a variety of mechanisms, including through face-to-face, two-way video, and Internet instruction. The effects of distance learning technologies on traditional structures of graduate education such as transfer of credit and residency have yet to be fully understood. However, new delivery methods certainly will affect overall demand, especially student demand for traditional site-based graduate education.

Implications for Institutional Researchers. Both colleges and universities will need to understand shifts in demand for graduate and professional school programs in order to fine-tune undergraduate programs so that they support the aspirations of their students. Universities will also need to understand these trends in order to manage their advanced-degree programs, including investments in plant and programs, staffing needs, and marketing requirements. Institutional researchers who seek to study these needs will have to work at two levels: (1) understanding national and regional trends in the demand for graduate and professional school courses and degree programs, and (2) assessing demand in an institution's specific markets and the institution's competitive position in attracting enrollments. In this concluding section, I discuss some resources for gaining these two types of intelligence.

National and Regional Enrollment Trends. As a first step, institutional researchers need to understand where their institution fits into the national graduate picture, and how the institution compares with peer institutions. Many of the sources cited in previous sections of this chapter are useful in this regard. Chief among the sources is the NCES Institutional Postsecondary Data System (IPEDS). The results of the IPEDS surveys are available in hard-copy, via the Internet on the NCES web page (http://www.ed.gov/NCES/), and recently in CD-ROM format. Baccalaureate and Beyond, a new longitudinal study from NCES on the transition from the bachelor's degree to career and advanced study, should provide institutional researchers insight into the decision process of students as they choose to enter the labor force and graduate and professional education.

Survey information focused on enrollment in science and engineering programs is available from the Division of Science Resources Studies of the National Science Foundation (http://www.nsf.gov/sbe/srs/stats.htm). The Council of Graduate Schools and the Graduate Record Examinations Board jointly conduct an annual survey of graduate enrollment, which includes data on applications and enrollment by field of study. The results of the CGS/GRE Survey of Graduate Enrollment are summarized in the annual publication, *Graduate Enrollment and Degrees* (Syverson and Welch, 1996).

The Bureau of the Census is the leading source of data on the upcoming demographic changes in the U.S. population. Those data are available at the national, state, and metropolitan area level. The P-25 report series (Day, 1996) provides published data on demographic trends, and these data are also available on the Internet (http://www.census.gov/population/).

The Bureau of Labor Statistics publishes perhaps the most useful information on occupational demands of the U.S. labor market in two publications—*Occupational Outlook Handbook, 1996–97* and *Employment Outlook: 1994–2005* (Bureau of Labor Statistics, 1995, 1996). These publications provide forecasts of the upcoming need for specific occupations, including descriptions of the educational requirements for jobs and the numbers of hires expected. Institutional researchers can use these data to provide a national picture of the potential job market for graduates of their institutions and the potential demand for graduate and professional level education.

While the Bureau of Labor Statistics provides data on labor market demand, the Annual Freshman Survey conducted by the Higher Education Research Institute provides data on another important piece of the demand picture—student interest in various fields of study. The results of the annual survey are published in *The American Freshman* (Sax, Astin, Korn, and Mahoney, 1995).

Assessing Demand in Specific Markets. The new demographics of graduate education make the assessment of demand in specific markets, and for specific institutions, especially challenging. Because of the nature of the adult population now entering graduate programs, surveys of enrolled students, for example of college seniors, are of limited value. Moreover, many students, especially those in master's degree programs, change majors between undergraduate and graduate study. There are three general techniques now being used to assess demand for individual institutions or programs: surveys of entering students including those that were admitted but declined to enroll, employer surveys, and use of commercial databases to target specific populations.

Surveys of Entering Students. A useful technique for assessing both the interest of students and the effectiveness of the institutional admissions process is to survey entering students, including those students who were accepted but chose to enter graduate study in another institution. Such surveys can include items focused on students' reasons for selecting the specific field of study and institution, cost and support issues, and how the institution fared in comparison with alternative universities. The survey of students who declined to attend can be especially illuminating in the area of competitiveness with peer institutions, and also can reveal important information about the admissions process. As an example, the Union Theological Seminary has developed surveys for both entering students and those declining the offer to attend. Tracking the results of those surveys over time has yielded useful information about student demand for Union graduate programs.

Employer Surveys. Many states now require that a survey of potential employers be conducted to demonstrate labor-market demand before new programs are approved. Often, institutions will work directly with employers in developing a new graduate program, thus assuring that there will be student demand for it. Employer surveys can be used to assess the education and training needs of public and private-sector employers in the service area of an institution. This technique is particularly useful when the graduate education-employer relationship is direct, as in professional areas such as health sciences, public administration, and elementary and secondary education.

Targeting Specific Populations. Assessing demand from specific populations using demographic-based marketing data is a technique commonly used by business but is relatively new to the graduate community. The American Marketing Association conducts an annual symposium on the Marketing of Higher Education, which includes sessions related to the marketing of graduate programs. One drawback to this technique is the cost involved in obtaining targeted marketing information, usually from commercial marketing firms. Lesley College has used this technique to identify individuals to participate in focus groups aimed at assessing expectations of graduate school and demand for various graduate programs.

Conclusion

Graduate education in the United States is entering an era of market segmentation, of varying student demand, and of changing requirements from employers. In the past, demand has come from traditional age cohorts who are able to attend on a full-time basis and from international students. In the new era, demand will come from older students, part-timers, and groups previously underrepresented in graduate education—women and members of minority groups.

This sea-change in graduate education will mean changes in the way students assess graduate opportunities and in the way institutions assess programs. Students will increasingly be interested in the outcomes of graduate education, looking beyond the degree credential to the impact on their careers. The increasing numbers of part-time and working adult students—coupled with the growing demand for professionally oriented graduate programs— raises questions about the traditional view of graduate education as preparation largely for a research or teaching career. This change, especially when combined with the much wider breadth of job opportunities and the increasing diversity of students, has important implications for graduate programs if they expect to meet new market demands in the years ahead. Additionally, those involved in graduate programs will have to reconsider how they assess programs and outcomes. Traditional measures of success, such as the number of graduates entering academe, will need to be broadened to reflect both the movement of advanced-degree recipients into new positions and the sustaining or enhancing of their current careers.

Notes

1. National data sources divide post-baccalaureate education into two broad categories, graduate and first-professional. Graduate programs include the physical sciences, biological and health sciences, engineering, social sciences, humanities, education, business, public administration, and other fields such as religion, architecture, and library science. First-professional fields include law, medicine, and dentistry.

2. Lomperis (1992) attributes much of the growth at the doctoral level to the growing pool of women baccalaureate recipients in the late 1960s and 1970s.

3. The NCES time-series data available on graduate enrollment by racial and ethnic group is not as complete as data for gender. NCES racial and ethnic data begins in 1976, and has years missing until 1990, when NCES began to collect such data on an annual basis.

4. Much of the early decrease in African American enrollment was due to a dramatic decrease in the number of black men enrolled in graduate education. Since 1988, however, the number of African American men has increased steadily. Carter and Wilson (1992) and Lomperis (1992) discuss the gender differences in higher education enrollment for African Americans.

5. Of course, many graduate students continue to take the traditional path of graduate study immediately following the baccalaureate. This is particularly the case in science and engineering doctoral programs.

PETER D. SYVERSON is vice president for research and information services at the Council of Graduate Schools, Washington, D.C.

*The authors discuss current admissions criteria, their validity in
predicting graduate student success, and a potentially more effective
model for predicting the success of various graduate student clienteles,
including women, minorities, and older students. Innovative
admissions criteria are also considered.*

Rethinking Admissions Criteria in Graduate and Professional Programs

Linda Serra Hagedorn, Amaury Nora

Graduate-level admissions decisions have important implications for both students and institutions. From the student's viewpoint, admission is a vital step toward career goal attainment. From an institutional perspective, each accepted student reflects the quality, reputation, and goals of the institution and the department. Faculty and administrators must make every effort, therefore, to adopt the most appropriate criteria that validly and accurately predict the selection of those students with a high likelihood of developing professional competencies and appropriate institutional fit, and who are likely to complete all degree requirements and to be satisfied with the program. The ability to acquire the specific skills needed to succeed in graduate and professional schools, however, may not be satisfactorily predicted through most traditional admissions criteria. Current admissions criteria that predict academic achievement in graduate and professional schools are no longer considered the sole criteria guiding admissions committees. Different and more current perspectives on what constitutes success in graduate schools now make it necessary to modify some indicators (or predictors) and identify new ones that relate to more varied and inclusive views of success.

The purpose of this chapter is to review the literature on various admissions criteria and to examine their validity in predicting both graduate student success (as traditionally defined) and the success of different graduate student clienteles, such as women, minorities, older students, arts and sciences students, and students in professional fields of study. A second discussion will focus on the need for alternative admissions criteria—a discussion based on the literature pertinent to differing views of student success in graduate and professional programs and suggested means for implementation. Finally, the chapter will include an examination of innovative admissions criteria used at graduate and professional schools around the country.

Predictive Validity of Existing Admissions Criteria

In general, graduate and professional schools require applicants to submit undergraduate transcripts, recent scores from a standardized aptitude test, an original essay (usually one addressing future goals), and letters of recommendation as part of the admissions process. At some institutions and in some departments, faculty may also require applicants to participate in an interview or render supplementary materials. The weights assigned to each of these criteria may vary by institution and department, but faculty typically place the most weight on minimum undergraduate overall grade point averages (Council of Graduate Schools, 1992) and standardized test scores when making admissions decisions.

Two basic assumptions underlie the use of undergraduate academic achievement and standardized achievement tests as predictors of subsequent success in graduate school: (1) success in an undergraduate program (defined as academic achievement) is predictive of academic achievement in graduate school, and (2) the behaviors and skills necessary for graduate work are merely an extension of the behaviors and skills that underlie success in undergraduate work. We examine each in turn.

Undergraduate Academic Achievement as Predictive of Graduate Achievement. Traditionally, faculty have used undergraduate grade point averages (GPAs) and standardized test scores to predict student achievement in graduate school. With few exceptions, tests of the predictive validity of these measures have used the first-year graduate GPA as the criterion (House, 1989; Kaczmarek and Franco, 1986; Matthews and Martin, 1992; Mitchell, Haynes, and Koenig, 1994; Thacker and Williams, 1974; Willingham, Lewis, Morgan, and Ramist, 1990; Wilson, 1982). The use of standardized test scores and undergraduate GPAs is troubling because of the inability of these two indicators to consistently and validly predict academic achievement beyond the first year (Arrow, 1993). In a recent meta-analysis of thirty published studies, Morrison and Morrison (1995) examined the validity of the Graduate Record Examination (GRE) to predict the first-year graduate GPA. Finding statistically nonsignificant correlation coefficients between first-year graduate GPA and GRE-verbal and GRE-quantitative scores, the authors concluded that the quantitative and verbal components of the GRE provide only minimal predictive validity. Additionally, other studies indicate that first-year grades are neither related to later graduate school grades nor to career performance (Arrow, 1993; Lipschutz, 1993) nor to persistence to degree completion (Girves and Wemmerus, 1988; Radin, Benbenishty, and Leon, 1982).

In addition to the limited applicability of undergraduate achievement and standardized tests scores in predicting first-year graduate academic achievement, researchers have found that these traditional admissions measures are biased against minorities and women. Even though testing organizations report the regular assessment of the reliability and validity of their standard admission tests, a history of test bias, as determined by the differential performances of individuals of different gender, race, socioeconomic status, and classification has continued (Vaseleck, 1994). The Office for Minority Education (1980) notes the adverse impact of standardized tests in a society with a historical pattern of differential treatment of minority students. Studies indicate that standardized tests underpredict aptitude for older students who may be hindered by their unfamiliarity with test-oriented environments (Brazziel, 1992; Clark, 1984; Swinton, 1987). Beyond test bias, test misuse introduces another threat to the validity of standardized test scores for admission purposes. For example, many admissions committees frequently combine GRE verbal, quantitative, and analytical scores into a single composite score of achievement or aptitude (Graduate Record Examinations Board, 1995). The Educational Testing Service (ETS) opposes this practice, on the grounds that each GRE component is designed to measure a different ability. For this reason, ETS advises graduate departments to consider the components individually in accordance with the skills and abilities believed to be important to graduate school success in specific fields (Graduate Record Examinations Board, 1995).

Test Bias and Minorities and Women. For years, researchers have reported that women and minorities (especially those from lower socioeconomic levels) do not perform as well as their white, male, middle-to-upper-class counterparts on standardized admission tests (Vaseleck, 1994). The use of standardized admission tests penalizes minority students, even though their undergraduate GPAs may not be different from those of nonminority students (Hartle, Baratz, and Clark, 1983; Pennock-Roman, 1990; Wilson, 1982). Moreover, Hathaway's (1984) study on Columbia University Law School students revealed not only that the Law School Admission Test (LSAT) had lower correlations with first-year grade point averages for females than for males but that the difference in the degree of relationship was much larger for third-year grades than for first-year grades. In the same study, Hathaway found that for a sample of minority students, the degree of association between LSAT and grades significantly dropped from the first year to the third year. The decrease in correlation for majority students was considerably smaller.

Even in studies where researchers found few significant differences in the degree of relationship between LSAT scores and first-year grades of minority and nonminority students, those few differences were further minimized when second- and third-year averages were considered. Pennock-Roman, for instance, found that the "grades of black and Chicano students improved much more than the grades for white students between their first and third years of law school. The mean difference in grades between minority and white students narrowed by the third year" (1986a, p. 248). The suggestion that differences in grades earned could be characteristic of minorities choosing to take easier courses was not substantiated. In a similar study, Powers (1986) concludes that "the differential improvements of minority students would seem to provide further justification to admitting minority and other disadvantaged students with lower admission credentials" (pp. 15–16).

Pennock-Roman's (1986b) research provides additional evidence of test bias in standardized tests for certain populations. When tests such as the *Prueba de Admision para Estudios Graduados* (PAEG)—an ETS admissions examination developed for the Graduate School Council of Puerto Rico—are constructed for specific populations, these tests appear to provide a substantial improvement over traditional versions of the Law School Admission Test (LSAT), the Admission Test for Graduate School in Business (ATGSB), and the Graduate Record Examination (GRE). One example of the improvement in the predictive ability of these tests appears in the validity coefficients found between the LSAT and first-year GPA in law school ($r = .39$) versus the PAEG and first-year GPA in law school ($r = .48$). While we do not advocate tailor-made standardized tests for every racial and ethnic group, our reading of the literature suggests that traditional standardized tests are biased against minorities and women and, as such, they should not be used as the only (or most influential) criteria in admissions selection decisions.

Other Factors Contributing to Test Bias. Several studies (Kirkland, 1971; Nairn, and Associates, 1980; Powers, 1986) have also found that extreme test anxiety may affect the performance of some students on standardized tests, thereby underpredicting their abilities. Research should seek to discover the factors that contribute to test anxiety and work to establish practical procedures that can reduce such anxiety or its negative effects (Powers, 1986).

Yet another current threat to the validity of the use of standardized tests is the availability of coaching schools that offer test preparation for a fee. The Federal Trade Commission and others report significant test score improvement when students participate in expensive coaching courses (Kulik, Bangert-Downs, and Kulik, 1984; Nairn, and Associates, 1980). Obviously, students who cannot afford the luxury of high-priced, test-tailored tutoring do not enjoy the same advantage as those who can.

Cognitive and Noncognitive Differences Between Graduate and Undergraduate Students. As stated earlier, the second basic assumption implicit in using undergraduate academic achievement as predictive of graduate GPA is that the behaviors and skills necessary for graduate work are merely an extension of the behaviors and skills that underlie success in undergraduate work. In other words, it is assumed that the cognitive and noncognitive experiences of undergraduates and graduates are similar and, therefore, past behaviors in an undergraduate environment would elicit similar behaviors in graduate school. Such an assumption is misguided; in contrast to undergraduates, most graduate students seek highly specialized knowledge, concentrate in one specific area, may be older, often come with extensive work experiences, are more certain of their goals and educational expectations, and are frequently impeded by adult and family responsibilities (Baird, 1993).

Moreover, individual experiences in graduate programs are very different from those in an undergraduate sequence. Whereas a substantial portion of the undergraduate program consists of general course work required of all students regardless of major, graduate study is very narrow and discipline-specific. In addition to obvious differences in content, graduate courses differ from undergraduate course work in character and style. Graduate courses are more likely than undergraduate courses to be taught in a seminar format, where students significantly contribute to the collective learning experience. Also, faculty hold graduate students to higher standards and frequently work side-by-side with them in research and related activities.

Faculty who focus only on selecting students with high undergraduate GPAs may exclude more mature students whose undergraduate records may not reflect their contemporary level of determination and promise (Hartle, Baratz, and Clark, 1983). Because a significant number of mature students enroll in graduate school after having had prior work experiences, many of these students have a better sense of their goals and educational commitments, which may have little relationship to undergraduate GPAs. Furthermore, learning is dynamic. Tests on the relationship between the learning ability of adults and age have concluded that although rapid increases in learning ability generally continue only into the early twenties, a slower yet sustained increase may extend until age sixty or beyond (Huppert and Kopelman, 1989; Knox, 1977). A denial of change or possible growth with regard to ability or motivation is inherent in the use of the traditional admissions criteria.

Success in Graduate and Professional Schools: An Alternative View

A recent report by ETS emphasizes the need for research on "variables other than test scores and undergraduate grade point average that would serve as better predictors of graduate degree completion for minority [and nonminority] graduate school applicants" (Brown, and others, 1994). Heeding the call of that report, in this section we introduce an alternative view of success in graduate and professional schools as a counterpoint to more traditional views that focus solely on academic achievement (graduate GPA). More specifically, we focus on expected outcomes of graduate preparation (as defined by degree program and discipline) and retention (degree completion) as two additional outcome measures of success.

Nature of Graduate Education. Enright and Gitomer (1989) note that "the very nature of [what constitutes] 'good performance' in graduate school is ill-defined. The process of graduate education is complex, variable, and often unstructured. Although admission to graduate school is based predominantly on measures of classroom performance or tests that predict classroom performance, evidence of potential professional distinction is typically exhibited and can be observed in situations outside the classroom" (p. 3). The basic premise in providing alternative definitions of success in graduate education is that the purpose of graduate education is to develop both professional and attitudinal competency. Success in graduate school, consequently, is viewed as the precursor of professional success. Enright and Gitomer note that "graduate school can be viewed as a work sample in which development as a student is equated with increasing approximation to professional behavior" (1989, p. 4).

Although academic achievement remains an indispensable measure of success in graduate education, other indicators of success—degree attainment, integration into the academic life of a department, professional involvement (engagement) in the chosen field of study, and career-related skills—deserve strong consideration at the graduate level. We believe that GPAs and standardized test scores cannot serve as accurate predictors of these types of student success. Different and more broad indicators of student success must be adopted, and more appropriate admissions criteria should be developed accordingly.

Competencies. Stark and her colleagues identified eleven major goals and outcomes for graduate professional students (Stark, Lowther, and Hagerty, 1986). These generic outcomes, divided into professional and attitudinal competencies, identify broad educational goals that extend beyond traditional academic achievement. Professional competencies refer to those skills, abilities, and proclivities that produce sound professional judgment and include conceptual, technical, contextual, interpersonal, integrative, and adaptive skills. In addition to these professional competencies, Stark and her colleagues found that outcomes pertaining to professional attitudes are equally important. These include career marketability, professional identity, ethical standards, scholarly concern for improvement, and motivation for continued learning.

While the development of professional and attitudinal competencies may be the goal of graduate education, two major questions arise: How are these competencies manifested? More importantly, How can they be predicted?

Participation in activities, events, and work that is related to a chosen discipline offers fertile ground for identifying students who have the potential to develop and demonstrate these professional competencies. In most instances, graduate applicants have had some experience in the field in which they are applying, either as paid workers or as volunteers. Even though the components of competency are defined by degree level and discipline, generally speaking, the ability to identify problems, deal with clients, plan investigations, write proposals, papers, and reports, participate and appropriately interact in professional networks, and critique the ideas, proposals, and work of others are examples of activities that may foreshadow eventual professional success. Participation in discipline-related apprenticeships may also be positively suggestive.

For students applying to a doctoral program, the importance of the prediction of scholarly engagement and research skills appears paramount. Nora, Cabrera, and Shinville (1994) examined the nature of academic growth and development and related scholarly behavior not only as the focus of theoretical models of graduate education but as an intended goal for doctoral students in most graduate programs and as the expected behavior by faculty. Scholarly engagement, from this vantage point, may be manifested in activities such as the presentation of a research paper at a professional conference, research with faculty, and attending meetings of professional organizations.

Although many of the desired outcomes for doctoral students appear mainly academic in nature, success in this arena additionally requires appropriate professional attitudes (such as career marketability, professional identity, ethical standards, scholarly concern for improvement, and motivation for continued learning). Attitude-related outcomes identified earlier by Stark and her colleagues (1986), along with academic predictors, may be most helpful in predicting successful students in a traditional doctoral program. Because our review of the literature revealed no empirical support for the validity of undergraduate GPAs or standardized test scores as predictors of student success in an attitudinal domain, other means for assessing this dimension appear warranted.

Retention. For some time now, the Council of Graduate Schools (1992) has clearly noted that "graduate admission policies and procedures should facilitate the matriculation of applicants who indicate *promise of successfully completing their chosen programs*" (p. 1, emphasis added). Retention, or degree completion, constitutes an incontestable aspect of success in graduate and professional education. In reviewing applications for graduate admission, one focus of the admissions committee should be the likelihood of potential students persisting to graduation. The importance of retention as an outcome is underscored by statistics that show that only half of all doctoral students persist until graduation (Baird, 1993; Bowen and Rudenstine, 1992; Tinto, 1993). The persistence rates for African American and Hispanic doctoral students are more alarming; only 30 to 40 percent eventually earn their degrees (Oliver and Brown, 1988; Sowell, 1989). Numerous studies on the persistence of students in graduate and professional schools establish retention as an outcome of extreme importance in graduate education, thereby meriting its inclusion as a measure of success.

Researchers have identified several factors that have an impact on graduate student persistence and completion. Regardless of the use of various comprehensive admissions criteria and the care with which prospective students are selected, persistence must be consistently nurtured through *mentoring* (Brazziel, 1984; Girves and Wemmerus, 1988; Thomas, Clewell, and Pearson, 1994), *academically and socially constructive faculty-student relationships* (Turner and Thompson, 1993; Williamson and Fenske, 1993), *professional development* (Nettles, 1990; Nettles, and others, 1986; Nora, Cabrera, and Shinville, 1994; Thomas, Clewell, and Pearson, 1992), and *financial support* (Ethington and Smart, 1986; Gillingham, Seneca, and Taussig, 1991; Trent and Copeland, 1987).

Conceptual Model of Success in Graduate Education. Most selection models for graduate school are based on a single assumption. According to Pennock-Roman (1986b):

There is one, unidimensional criterion Y, such as college grade-point average (C-GPA), that measures "success.". . . A predictor X exists, which can be a linear combination of variables, that has demonstrable validity for estimating Y in advance. The various models differ in how they specify that acceptance or cutting scores on X be derived in order to decide who scores high enough on X in

order to be admitted. Since the relationship between predictors and the criterion is far from perfect, some selection decisions will turn out to be correct pre-
classifications of candidates, and others will turn out to be errors. [p. 252]

Figure 3.1 presents a proposed conceptual framework that provides an alternative view to most traditional models. The model incorporates new measures
or outcomes associated with "success" in graduate school, along with traditional measures. The model identifies factors found to have an impact on both
traditional (academic achievement as measured by GPA) and nontraditional
(professional competencies, attitudinal competencies, and retention) measures
of success. Finally, the model links those factors associated with different measures of success with traditional (undergraduate GPA, standardized tests) and
nontraditional (interviews, critiques, reports, unstandardized instruments)
admissions criteria.

Figure 3.1. Conceptual Framework

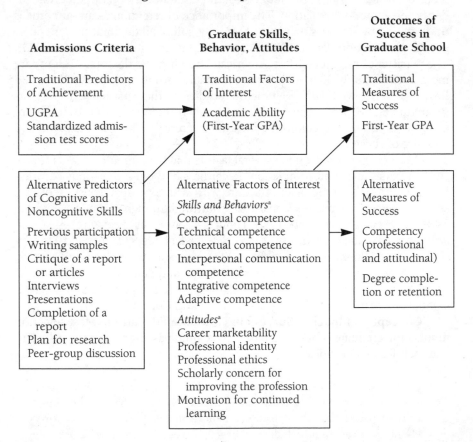

Admissions Criteria	Graduate Skills, Behavior, Attitudes	Outcomes of Success in Graduate School
Traditional Predictors of Achievement UGPA Standardized admis- sion test scores	Traditional Factors of Interest Academic Ability (First-Year GPA)	Traditional Measures of Success First-Year GPA
Alternative Predictors of Cognitive and Noncognitive Skills Previous participation Writing samples Critique of a report or articles Interviews Presentations Completion of a report Plan for research Peer-group discussion	Alternative Factors of Interest *Skills and Behaviors*[a] Conceptual competence Technical competence Contextual competence Interpersonal communication competence Integrative competence Adaptive competence *Attitudes*[a] Career marketability Professional identity Professional ethics Scholarly concern for improving the profession Motivation for continued learning	Alternative Measures of Success Competency (professional and attitudinal) Degree comple- tion or retention

[a] Adapted from Stark, Lowther, and Hagerty, 1986

Specifically, the model displays the relationships among admissions criteria, graduate skills, behaviors, and attitudes, and outcomes of success in graduate schools. The first block identifies both traditional and alternative admissions criteria. The second block in the framework represents the goals (skills, behaviors, and attitudes) of graduate and professional education. The third and final block represents measurable outcomes of success in graduate school, as defined both traditionally and as proposed.

Relationship Between Factors, Outcome Measures, and the Admissions Process. As displayed in Figure 3.1, traditional measures of admissions criteria do not provide the means for capturing the skills, behaviors, and attitudes that researchers have linked to success in graduate school. For instance, both undergraduate GPA and standardized tests are measures of a cognitive dimension that excludes professional and attitudinal competency.

The proposed framework sheds light on links between predictors of desired graduate outcomes (skills, behaviors, and attitudes developed in graduate education) and measures (both traditional and alternative) of graduate success. It should be noted that although there have been numerous tests of the validity of standardized admission tests (using first-year GPA as the criterion), alternative measures of success incorporated in the conceptual framework have not been empirically tested. However, there is some preliminary evidence that these activities, separately or together with standardized admission tests, provide important and useful information in the assessment of graduate school applicants.

Enright and Gitomer (1989) propose a systematic approach for assessing the probability of students' success in graduate school more broadly conceived. In a report to the ETS, they describe a framework for linking competencies expected of graduate students with specific exercises (or techniques-procedures). Their approach can be used to craft alternative indicators for admissions purposes. The authors identify five exercises that can be used to provide information on an applicant's suitability for graduate school. The exercises include conducting structured background interviews, completing a report, critiquing a paper or report, planning further research, and holding peer-group discussions. They recommend these five exercises as possible admission screening devices.

In the structured interviews, for example, admissions committees can gather information about applicants' research interests, previous academic and nonacademic experiences and achievements, and sources of enjoyment and satisfaction. As Enright and Gitomer (1989) explain:

> This task is viewed as most appropriate for the applicant or entering student. Often, the expectations of the beginning graduate student and the reality of graduate school and the profession are inconsistent. This lack of congruity often has deleterious effects on student motivation. Also, students may not apportion their resources in optimal fashion (Sternberg, 1985). Therefore, assessment information from this task can be used in two ways. First, students who do not have a

realistic view of graduate school can decide on the basis of feedback whether or
not such an environment suits their needs. Similarly, student search committees
can use the information in an analogous fashion. [p. 18]

A recent study of medical school admissions practices adds additional support
to the use of admission interviews. This study found admission interview ratings to be predictive of third- and fourth-year medical school performance (as
measured by GPAs) (Elam and Johnson, 1992).

Asking an applicant to critique a report or paper likewise can be used to
assess applicants' abilities to plan, communicate in writing, synthesize information, and devise explanations for findings. This alternative admissions approach may also provide the admissions committee with evidence of the
creativity or resourcefulness of the applicant. Another attractive feature of this
activity is that it can easily be administered through mail or through electronic
means. Enright and Gitomer (1989) state that "such an exercise has relevance
throughout the graduate and professional career. A researcher in almost any
discipline must be able to synthesize and interpret information, as well as offer
and communicate explanations for such a set of findings" (p. 18). The authors
caution, however, that the level of knowledge admissions committees seek of
applicants should not be so specific that it favors a subset of individuals who
have had special exposure to relevant material over others.

As part of the selection process, admissions committees could also ask applicants to plan a research study. Students would be required to identify issues
or questions for investigation, suggest possible methods for studying those
issues, specify the kinds of evidence that would be relevant, anticipate possible outcomes, and suggest likely explanations for alternative outcomes. Similar to the previous exercise, this exercise can also be easily administered to
students. This exercise would provide evidence of students' planning, synthesis, and creativity skills.

Finally, Enright and Gitomer recommend peer-group discussions that
could provide measures of numerous competencies in students. This activity,
however, may require extensive planning by admissions committees. Enright
and Gitomer acknowledge that using such an approach for admissions purposes may be unwieldy. They suggest this exercise be used to assess students'
skills upon matriculation. Problems associated with the standardization of
group discussions also limit the use of this technique in the selection process.

Innovative Admissions Criteria at Different Graduate and Professional Programs

We recently requested information on innovative graduate admissions criteria
from institutions and departments across the country through two Internet listservs. Both listservs are available to members of the American Educational
Research Association (AERA). The first listserv, AERA-J, is open to members of
division J (post-secondary education) and as of May, 1996, serves 864 sub-

scribers. The second listserv, AERA-D, serves members of Division D (research design and methodology) and presently serves 1,120 subscribers. We requested information on departments using nontraditional criteria in admitting applicants to their graduate programs. We specified that we were interested in criteria used either in addition to or instead of traditional methods. In response to our query, we received twenty responses identifying fourteen institutions with innovative graduate admissions criteria. In each case, the admissions office of the institution was contacted, as were key faculty who could verify and clarify practiced procedures. In all cases, personnel reported the new methods superior to the more traditional ones previously used. In this section, we discuss some of the alternative criteria and methods and relate them to the conceptual framework described earlier. Our intent is to link alternative criteria used by admissions committees to the factors and outcome measures identified in the conceptual framework. Because these methods have not been empirically tested, evidence of their utility is purely anecdotal. The need for comprehensive inquiry by institutional research professionals is very apparent.

In addition to those institutions identified through our Internet queries, we contacted several graduate admissions personnel in various institutions throughout the United States and Canada that we chose at random. Our inquiries indicated that departments in the hard, pure, and life disciplines tend to rely on traditional admissions criteria more than departments whose disciplines can be classified as soft, applied, or nonlife (see Biglan 1973a and 1973b for a description of discipline classifications). We found the majority of departments using alternative admissions criteria in the social sciences. Among those departments, several no longer require any standardized test scores, and some have established no absolute cut-off scores. However, when test scores are found to be low, admissions committees often consider higher GPAs, membership in a nontraditional age group, or underrepresented ethnic or racial group as additional considerations in the admissions decision.

Differential Weighting of Factors. Faculty in the doctoral program in Educational Leadership at Arkansas State University use an elaborate, weighted criteria formula to assess applicants' academic promise and leadership potential. The formula examines academic ability, conceptualization and research skills, and evidence of commitment and professionalism. Although academic ability is highly considered, the emphasis on scholarship and professional promise makes this admission scheme nontraditional. Specific weights or percentages (points) are assigned to different criteria and incorporated as part of an intricate procedure that involves all departmental faculty in the final admissions decision.

Following are the weights assigned to admissions criteria: *academic ability* (30 percent), including undergraduate GPA (15 percent) and a Miller Analogies test score (15 percent); *scholarship* (30 percent), including written expression, as assessed through formal papers, original works, and publications (20 percent) and a personal statement (10 percent); *professional promise* (40 percent), including an assessment of leadership potential, as determined from letters of recommendation, membership in professional organizations, offices held, honors received, and other professional achievements (10 percent), academic readiness, as measured on the basis of past degrees, certification, completed course work, as well as deficiencies (10 percent), appropriateness of work experience (10 percent), and compatibility of professional goals and aspirations with the program's mission (10 percent).

Completed application files are circulated to the faculty for ratings. Each faculty member in the department assigns a score between minus 4 and plus 4 (zero is the midpoint) for each category. Applicants must score at least 100 points to be invited for an interview.

The approach by Arkansas State focuses on academic achievement, aptitude, and attitudes, as previously presented in the conceptual framework. Faculty at this institution believe that the addition of components beyond tests of academic ability has been very beneficial. In the words of a faculty member, "We have admitted students with MATs in the 55–70 range who turn out to be absolute dogs; conversely, we have admitted students with scores below freezing who have performed well in the program and as leaders in the field."

Construction of a Portfolio. At the Center for Teaching and Learning at the University of North Dakota, faculty have crafted admissions criteria congruent with the philosophy of their program. As stated in the college catalogue, faculty seek to admit students who have "the qualities of creativity, intelligence, independence of thought, willingness to take risks, openness to new ideas, openness to diversity, . . . flexibility of thought, . . . commitment to learners of all ages, professional growth, self-direction, and commitment to academic study leading to a graduate degree" (gopher://sage.und.nodak.edu:70/00/acad_prog/cat/grinfo/ersprog/educ/admreq). Admissions criteria and the selection process represent a holistic approach in admissions procedures. The different criteria provide measures of an applicant's "habits of mind."

In addition to undergraduate transcripts, applicants are required to construct a portfolio that includes a completed application form and a personal statement of goals, characteristics, attitudes, values, skills, and past accomplishments. Also included are appropriate supplemental materials such as publications and a detailed description of a day in the applicant's classroom or professional setting. A personal interview (either in person or by telephone) is also required.

Two-Tier Admissions Process. The doctoral program in higher education at Texas A & M University uses a two-tier admissions process. Students with appropriate GRE scores, undergraduate GPAs, and those whose initial writing sample meets admissions standards are required to make a ten-to-fifteen-minute presentation to the faculty from a previously received list of topics. This procedure permits faculty to observe communication and explanation skills and the professionalism of prospective students.

Students judged acceptable in the first tier are invited back to interview with a representative sample of faculty from the higher education department. At that time, students are also asked to write a brief essay. Faculty use this writing sample to assess further the applicants' writing, organization, and conceptualization skills.

Group Interviews. Admission to the master's program in educational administration at Seattle University requires no standardized test scores. As one faculty member in the program told us: "We've given up on GREs, because we couldn't tell that those who did really well on them operated any better than those who were barely at the passing level for admission at the time." Undergraduate GPA is used to assess future academic achievement.

To assess the attitudes and aptitudes of applicants as specified in the conceptual framework, this on-site interview is mandatory. Faculty hold group interviews approximately once a month with "whoever shows up." In addition, research and writing skills of Ed.D. applicants are assessed through a thirty-minute, on-site synthesis and analysis of two articles on a similar topic.

Conclusion

Specifying appropriate graduate admissions criteria is not an easy task. While it is easier to list the many factors related to the successful retention and acquisition of outcomes in graduate education, three questions still remain: Can interviews, student statements, letters, critiques, departmental tests, or other vehicles accurately and efficiently measure whether a potential graduate student will be successful in earning an advanced degree? Can these exercises and tasks better predict successful engagement in activities supported and valued by the field? Will alternative admissions methods be less biased against nontraditional applicants than present admissions criteria?

It is possible that admissions committees can assess educational aspirations, motivation, a propensity for scholarly work, and a positive attitude for collaborative work through a personal interview, statements provided by the applicant, or even a student survey. It is even possible to attain information on a student's financial circumstances, his or her yearning to integrate fully not only into the academic life of a department but into a chosen profession as well.

What is problematic are the ethical and pragmatic issues raised as a consequence of using alternative admissions criteria directly related to factors exerting an effect on different measures of success. Are graduate schools to select from only those students that fit a restrictive profile of a potentially successful graduate student? If the literature indicates that attending full-time, having a high GPA, having certain educational aspirations and motivation, and having a desire for a scholarly career leads to success, does that mean that students who cannot afford to attend on a full-time basis, are not as highly motivated as others, and have no interest in academia nor in seeking an academic appointment should be denied admission to graduate school? Would that not exclude those who wish to acquire the knowledge and skills to become effective practitioners? Would that not also exclude highly motivated students who cannot attend full-time because of financial commitments?

Moreover, the costs (both financial and in time) associated with the adoption and use of alternative admissions methods must also be considered. Although the methods presented require much more faculty time than traditional methods, we believe the benefits to faculty, the institution, and applicants are worthwhile. As graduate admissions criteria are assessed and reevaluated, a workable solution may lie in striking a balance on the indicators of student success outlined in this chapter.

Notes

1. The address of the AERA listserv is listserv@asuvm.inre.asu.edu or listserv@asuacad.-bitnet

2. The Biglan classification scheme is three-dimensional. The first dimension, hard/soft, classifies disciplines by "subject matter characteristics and department organization" (Malaney, 1986, p. 85). The second dimension, pure/applied, separates disciplines into those which emphasize pure research and those that emphasize practical applications. The third dimension categorizes disciplines on their involvement with living structures. See Malaney (1986) for more information on and examples of this classification scheme.

LINDA SERRA HAGEDORN is assistant professor at the Center for Higher Education Policy Analysis at the University of Southern California.

AMAURY NORA is professor of higher education at the University of Houston.

A theory of program quality is presented that is centered around a new definition of quality. Constructed on the basis of interviews with nearly eight hundred stakeholders in master's-level education, the theory advances a conceptual template and a set of criteria for assessing program quality in graduate and professional education.

Refocusing Quality Assessment on Student Learning

Jennifer Grant Haworth, Clifton F. Conrad

What is a high-quality graduate program? How do we know a "quality" program when we see one? What specific criteria do we use to render such judgments, and how confident are we that they are valid measures of quality? Do we have a sturdy empirical foundation that justifies our definitions and the standards we use in assessing quality?

In this chapter, we draw upon the program quality literature and our own research on quality in graduate education to address these questions. In so doing, we argue that contemporary views of quality have been premised on a "prestige" model that "stoke[s] academic egos instead of students' dreams" (Association of Governing Boards, 1992, p. 22).

We organize our argument into three sections. To place our ideas in context, we begin by outlining five views of program quality that can be found in the literature, and we discuss their limitations. Then, in light of these shortcomings, we advance a new view of program quality—a learning-centered view—that places student learning at the center of our understanding of program quality. Finally, and grounded in this learning-centered view, we discuss a recently developed theory of quality that has the potential to refocus quality assessment in graduate education on student learning. This theory provides faculty, administrators, institutional researchers, and others with an innovative set of quality attributes and indicators that can inform and guide their quality assessment efforts.

Views of Quality

In a recent review of more than one hundred research studies, scholarly essays, and books on quality in higher education, we identified five prevailing views

NEW DIRECTIONS FOR INSTITUTIONAL RESEARCH, no. 92, Winter 1996 © Jossey-Bass Publishers of program quality in the higher education literature (Haworth and Conrad, 1997). The five views are *faculty,* resources, student quality and effort, curriculum requirements, and *multidimensional-multilevel.* We will briefly discuss each of these views, their attributes, and shortcomings.

The first three views—the faculty, resources, and student quality-and-effort views—are familiar to anyone who has even a passing familiarity with higher education. In brief, these views suggest that program quality can be reduced to one of the following five propositions.

Proposition One. The quality of an academic program can be judged by the quality of its faculty. That is, a high-quality program has faculty who have completed their doctoral training under the guidance of recognized scholars at highly regarded research universities, are actively engaged in research and publication (frequently as measured by numbers of publications and citation counts), have secured external funding to support their research programs, and are recognized nationally by their peers as able and productive scholars (Blackburn and Lingenfelter, 1973; Conrad and Blackburn, 1986; Fairweather and Brown, 1991; King and Wolfe, 1987).

Proposition Two. The quality of an academic program can be judged by the quality of its students. That is, a high-quality program is one that attracts students with outstanding undergraduate academic records and superior standardized test scores who, upon matriculation, devote significant and sustained efforts to their studies (the latter is often measured by Robert Pace's student quality and effort scale) (Astin, 1977, 1993; Conrad and Blackburn, 1985a; Kuh, 1981; Pace, 1980, 1986).

Proposition Three. The quality of an academic program can be judged by the quantity of its resources. That is, a high-quality program is one that has a critical mass of faculty and students, solid financial resources, and excellent physical facilities (including laboratories, computers, classrooms, and library resources) (Cartter, 1966; Conrad and Blackburn, 1986; Fairweather, 1988; Fairweather and Brown, 1991; Jones, Lindzey, and Coggeshall, 1982).

Proposition Four. The quality of an academic program can be judged by the rigor of its curricular requirements. Specifically, a high-quality program is one that requires students to complete a prescribed set of course work, an on-campus residency, and a culminating experience—such as a comprehensive examination, master's thesis, or doctoral dissertation (Conrad and Wilson, 1985; Council of Graduate Schools, 1981; Glazer, 1986).

Proposition Five. The quality of an academic program can be judged by the relative strength of its faculty, students, resources, and curricular requirements. That is, a high-quality program is multidimensional (in contrast to the unidimensional views of quality described previously) and provides evidence of that quality across key dimensions of excellence (Blackburn and Lingenfelter, 1973; Clark, 1976; Clark, Hartnett, and Baird, 1976; Conrad and Blackburn, 1985b; Fairweather and Brown, 1991; Jones, Lindzey, and Coggeshall, 1982; Kuh, 1981).

These views provide a foundation for understanding contemporary conceptions of program quality in American higher education. During the past twenty-five years, several scholars have studied many attributes associated with these views, including those related to faculty, students, and resources. These studies, referred to as "studies of the quantitative attributes of quality" (Conrad and Blackburn, 1986), have attempted to isolate program-related attributes that explain the greatest amount of variation in departments assumed to be of high-quality (as measured most frequently by peers' reputational rankings). Over the years, scholars working in this vein have identified positive relationships between program quality so measured, and measures of the following: *faculty educational training* (Clemente and Sturgis, 1974; Conrad and Blackburn, 1985a; Crane, 1970); *faculty scholarly productivity*, such as the mean number of research articles and books (Abbott and Barlow, 1972; Conrad and Blackburn, 1985a; Drew and Karpf, 1981); *program size*, as measured by the number of faculty and students (Abbott, 1972; Conrad and Blackburn, 1986; Fairweather, 1988; Fairweather and Brown, 1991; Oromaner, 1970); *institutional and programmatic financial resources* (Abbott and Barlow, 1972; Beyer and Snipper, 1974; Lavendar, Mathers, and Pease, 1971; Morgan, Kearney, and Regens, 1976); and various *measures of student selectivity and ability* (Conrad and Blackburn, 1985a; Hagstrom, 1971).

Limitations. At first glance, there appears to be a sturdy foundation of empirical knowledge lending support to these views of quality. Yet, upon close examination, we identified five major shortcomings in the literature that raise serious questions about these extant views.

First, the validity of the empirical research supporting current views of program quality is very much in doubt, in large part because most researchers have used reputational rankings as the measure of program quality. Several authors have argued that reputational rankings have severe limitations as measures of program quality (Clark, 1976; Conrad and Blackburn, 1985b; Conrad and Pratt, 1985; Fairweather, 1988; Lawrence and Green, 1980; Webster, 1981, 1986a, 1986b). Perhaps the most important of these is that reputational rankings rate only those programs and departments in highly visible research universities (thereby ignoring most institutions of higher education in the United States) and, in so doing, focus far more attention on measuring visibility and prestige than quality, per se. Hence, reputation has come to serve as a rather dubious criterion for quality in many of these studies.

Second, many of the attributes included under each of these views of quality—including student board scores, a thesis requirement, or library holdings, for example—have been identified and tested exclusively on an atheoretical basis. That is, in trying to get a handle on what program quality is, most researchers have selected, a priori, those program features that they predicted would correlate positively with programs assumed to be of high quality. In essence, since scholars have concentrated primarily on finding positive correlations between selected program characteristics and the measure of their dependent variable—highly ranked programs—our knowledge of quality attributes is both atheoretical and misleading. From our perspective, the research tells us far more about attributes of program prestige than attributes of high-quality programs.

Third, for the most part, current views of quality tend to focus on "input" or "output" features of graduate programs. While useful as far as they go, these views fail to identify or explain how features within the "black box" of programs contribute to student learning (Kuh, 1992, p. 354). That is, they fail to give faculty and administrators insights into what they could do to enhance student learning while students are enrolled in their programs.

Fourth, and closely linked to the previous limitations, many of our current views of quality—and the attributes they embrace and consequently promote—have not been found to have significant connections to student learning, growth, and development. In their recent synthesis of the literature on how college affects students, Patrick Terenzini and Ernest Pascarella (1994) cast doubt on the salience of many attributes that researchers have upheld as hallmarks of a high-quality program.[1] In their words:

> After taking into account the characteristics, abilities, and backgrounds students bring with them to college, we found that how much students grow or change has only inconsistent and, perhaps in a practical sense, trivial relationships with such traditional measures of institutional "quality" as educational expenditures per student, student/faculty ratios, faculty salaries, percentage of faculty with the highest degree in their field, faculty research productivity, size of the library, admissions selectivity, or prestige rankings. [p. 29]

Terenzini and Pascarella's conclusion is a damning one that should make any faculty member or administrator who is concerned about quality take notice. After all, even if scholars have identified many so-called quality attributes, just how valuable is that knowledge if the empirical evidence fails to show that these attributes have important effects on student learning?

Fifth, the five views of program quality represented in the literature have, for the most part, been based on the perspectives of a limited range of stakeholders—usually scholars, senior administrators, and faculty—at highly visible research universities and institutes. As a result, we have developed an understanding of program quality that has failed to include the perspectives of administrators and faculty at less prestigious universities, or those of students, alumni, or employers across all types of institutions. Most certainly, these stakeholders—all of whom are directly involved with graduate and professional programs—have views on program quality that merit attention and study.

To summarize, after critically examining myriad research studies, essays, and books on program quality in higher education, we identified five prevailing views of quality in the literature. Numerous limitations aside, these views—and the attributes that accompany them—have strongly influenced how faculty, administrators, and institutional researchers currently approach, define, and assess graduate program quality. Curiously, these views have become deeply entrenched in higher education, despite mounting evidence that they provide little usable information on program quality, particularly as it relates to student learning. If faculty and administrators are truly committed to improving the quality of their graduate and professional programs, we need a new view of quality—one that will make learners and learning central in our discussions and evaluations of program quality. Such a new view will, as the Association of Governing Boards of Universities and Colleges (1992) states, emphasize the development of high-quality academic programs that focus first on "realizing students' dreams" (p. 22).

Learning-Centered View of Program Quality

We must, as the Wingspread Group on Higher Education (1993) has implored, put student learning first in our discussions of program quality in higher education. For far too long, individuals both within and outside the academy have divorced their understandings of program quality from broader questions of student learning. In this section, we argue that the academy needs a learning-centered view of quality. Such a view will challenge faculty, administrators, and institutional researchers to ensure that "every activity, every action, every resource [be] directed toward students and, more generally, toward [the] maximization of learning for every constituency" in our nation's colleges and universities (Bergquist, 1995, p. 65).

We provide the conceptual groundwork for a learning-centered view of quality in *Emblems of Quality in Higher Education: Developing and Sustaining High-Quality Programs* (Haworth and Conrad, 1997). We anchor our view in a definition of high-quality programs as those that, from the perspective of diverse stakeholders, provide enriching learning experiences for students that have positive effects on students' growth and development. This definition places student learning at the center of all efforts to understand, improve, and assess program quality in higher education.

Why define high-quality programs in terms of students' learning? Perhaps the most compelling reason is a simple one: student development is the raison d'etre of higher education. Particularly in recent years, a growing number of scholars and policy analysts have stepped forward to emphasize and defend the fundamental importance of student learning in the academy (Astin, 1985; Barr and Tagg, 1995; Chickering and Gamson, 1987; Guskin, 1994; Kuh, Schuh, and Whitt, 1991; and Sanford, 1968). Similarly, several major policy-making bodies (American College Personnel Association, 1994; Study Group, 1984; Wingspread Group, 1993) have also defended student learning as the signature responsibility of our nation's colleges and universities.

From our perspective, a learning-centered view of program quality provides a new vantage point for understanding and evaluating quality in graduate education. Rather than defining and assessing quality in terms of where a particular program stands in relation to others (an externally directed, competitive starting point that all too frequently emphasizes comparative quality standards focused far more on assessing prestige than quality), a learning-centered view begins by examining how the inner workings of a particular program enhance or diminish student learning experiences and outcomes (an internally directed, formative starting point that stresses quality standards focused primarily on student learning). Such a view focuses attention on the relationships between what actually goes on inside academic programs and how myriad actions affect student learning in important ways. This latter view, we believe, has the potential to provide faculty, administrators, and institutional researchers with keen insights into, and usable information on, graduate program quality on their campuses.

Refocusing Quality Assessment on Student Learning

What might a high-quality graduate program look like if we constructed it around a learning-centered view of quality? What distinctive program features, or attributes, would distinguish the program from others, and how would these attributes affect students' learning experiences and outcomes? In this section, we present our research on high-quality graduate programs, defined as those that, from the perspective of diverse stakeholders, provide enriching learning experiences to students—experiences that have positive effects on students' growth and development (Haworth and Conrad, 1997). Specifically, we introduce our newly developed theory of quality—a theory, we believe, that has strong potential for refocusing quality assessment in graduate and professional education on student learning.

Engagement Theory of Quality. Over the past several years, we have focused our research on developing a theory of quality in higher education. Building on our learning-centered definition of a high-quality program—and grounded in the perspectives of the nearly eight hundred faculty, administrators, students, alumni, and employers we interviewed associated with forty-seven master's programs in thirty-one institutions across the nation—the theory identifies seventeen characteristics, or attributes, of programs that contribute to enriching learning experiences for students that positively affect their growth and development. The theory not only describes a number of attributes associated with high-quality programs, it also provides an explanatory basis for understanding how and why these attributes enhance student learning experiences and outcomes.

Drawing on what we learned from these individuals about high-quality learning experiences, we systematically identified and knitted together attributes—and clusters of attributes—into a unified theory of program quality. Using the constant comparative method (Glaser and Strauss, 1967) to analyze our interview material, we constructed an "engagement theory" that describes an ideal high-quality master's program. None of the programs in our sample had all seventeen of the attributes included in the theory.

We organized our theory of program quality around one central idea: student, faculty, and administrative engagement in teaching and learning. In our study, we learned that high-quality programs are those in which students, faculty, and administrators invest significant time and effort in mutually supportive teaching and learning. Students invest in teaching as well as learning, and faculty and administrators invest in learning as well as teaching (Haworth and Conrad, 1997). Additionally, faculty and administrators encourage program alumni and employer involvement in their programs. At its most fundamental level, then, the engagement theory accentuates the pivotal role that participants play in developing and sustaining programs of high quality that promote mutually supportive teaching and learning.

More specifically, the theory holds that in high-quality programs, faculty, students, and administrators invest in five separate clusters of program attributes, each of which contributes to enriching learning experiences for students that positively affect students' growth and development. The five clusters of program attributes are *diverse and engaged participants, participatory cultures, interactive teaching and learning, connected program requirements,* and *adequate resources.* Table 4.1 provides a partial summary of the engagement theory (see Haworth and Conrad, 1997, pp. 31–39, for a capsule summary of the entire theory, including the positive effects that each attribute has on students' growth and development).

To familiarize readers with the theory, we will briefly touch upon a few of its unique attributes.

Diverse and Engaged Participants. Throughout our study, we became increasingly aware that the most important animating force in high-quality programs is diverse and engaged participants. As the people who take responsibility for teaching and learning, these participants play a pivotal role in enhancing the quality of learning experiences that students have in graduate programs.

Perhaps because it provides an interesting contrast to prevailing views of faculty quality discussed in the literature, the first attribute in this cluster—diverse and engaged faculty—bears special mention here. Many interviewees told us that while conventional quality criteria for faculty, such as educational preparation and scholarly productivity, were important, they stressed that two other faculty attributes—diversity and engagement—substantially enhanced the overall quality of students' learning experiences in their programs. Diversity, in this instance, refers to the range of scholarly and experiential perspectives that faculty infuse into their teaching. Engagement refers to the investments that faculty make in their students' learning, devoting time and energy to classroom preparation and teaching, as well as to various out-of-class activities, including supervising independent studies, directing student theses, and working with students on collaborative research and service-related projects.

Across our sample, interviewees underscored the important role that diverse and engaged faculty play in developing and sustaining high-quality programs. Perhaps a faculty member-turned-executive best expressed the centrality of this attribute when he said:

Table 4.1. Overview of Engagement Theory

Attribute	Consequences for Learning Experiences
Cluster One: *Diverse and Engaged Participants*	
Diverse and Engaged Faculty	Faculty infuse diverse perspectives into their classroom lectures, discussions, and out-of-class interactions with students.
	Faculty dedicate significant time and energy to teaching, including outside-of-class involvement with students.
Diverse and Engaged Students	Students contribute fresh perspectives to discussions they have with one another and with faculty.
	Students invest time and energy in their own and others' learning through active participation in formal and informal learning activities.
	Leaders effectively promote their program to internal and external audiences and are adept at securing resources to sustain it.
Engaged Leaders	Leaders attract and support diverse and engaged faculty and students.
	Leaders encourage participants to assume informal program leadership roles.
Cluster Two: *Participatory Cultures*	
Shared Program Direction	Stakeholders share an overall program direction that both informs and animates their actions and provides a common thread that knits together students' learning experiences.
Community of Learners	Participants experience their program as a "learning community" in which faculty and students teach and learn from one another, more or less as colleagues.
	Participants experience camaraderie among and between faculty and students that supports and complements the overall sense of community.
Risk-Taking Environment	Supported and challenged to take risks, students regularly question orthodoxies, advance alternative perspectives and approaches, and engage in learning activities that press the boundaries of their potential.

Cluster Three: Interactive Teaching and Learning

Critical Dialogue

Faculty and students engage in disciplined and mutually enriching dialogue in which they constantly question one another, examine assumptions and differing points of view, and generate critically informed understandings of knowledge and professional practice.

Integrative Learning: Theory with Practice, Self with Subject

Students participate in learning activities in which they connect theoretical and applied knowledge to complex problems, issues, and situations in the real world.

Mentoring

Students receive individualized advice, guidance, and feedback from faculty in various ways: working together in the lab, field, or studio, in formal meetings, and through informal interactions.

Cooperative Peer Learning

Students participate in group activities in which they contribute to and support one another's learning in ways that enrich their understanding of knowledge and professional practice.

Out-of-Class Activities

Students—and occasionally faculty—participate in a variety of informal, out-of-class activities in which they explore topics of mutual interest and enrich one another's learning.

Cluster Four: Connected Program Requirements

Planned Breadth and Depth

Students complete a combination of core and specialized course work in which they gain both generalized and specialized knowledge.

Professional Residency

Residential learning experiences challenge students to build bridges between what they learn in classes and what they encounter in real-world settings, thereby helping them to develop a more robust and connected understanding of their professions.

Tangible Product

In developing a tangible product, students are challenged to draw upon and knit together relevant principles, practices, and skills that they have learned in their programs to create a product that is of value to the field, as well as to them personally.

Table 4.1. Overview of Engagement Theory (*continued*)

Attribute	Consequences for Learning Experiences
Cluster Five: Adequate Resources	
Support for Students	Students who receive financial aid for full-time study or who complete their studies part-time in programs with nontraditional delivery formats are in a better position to concentrate on their learning. Students who take advantage of career counseling and job placement services learn job-search strategies and develop professional networks that better prepare them for locating employment upon graduation.
Support for Faculty	When faculty are adequately supported, they invest significant time and effort in teaching and mentoring students.
Support for Basic Infrastructure	When basic infrastructure needs are met, students are in a better position to learn advanced knowledge and techniques.

Source: Haworth and Conrad, 1997, pp. 31–39. Used by permission of Allyn & Bacon.

Within every university that I've been associated with, it's the compassion of the faculty and the leadership—it's the faculty that care about the students . . . that makes all the difference. . . . It doesn't matter how you design the program on paper. If it's not executed by faculty advisors, by faculty willing to take students into the lab and provide the research training experience, by faculty who teach the courses [then an essential quality link is missing].

Participatory Program Cultures. Our research also indicates that participatory program cultures are an important feature of high-quality programs. As we came to understand, faculty, administrators, and students who are serious about quality actively seek to develop and sustain collegial and supportive cultures through the creation of a shared program direction, involvement in a community of learners, and participation in a risk-taking learning environment. We briefly describe the first and third attributes here.

Most of us are probably familiar with the adage, "If you don't know where you're going, you'll probably end up somewhere else." In our study, a clearly stated and widely understood program direction emerged as a distinctive feature of high-quality programs, one that frequently gives participants an integrative thread to knit together meaningful teaching and learning experiences for students. During a site visit to an environmental studies program, for instance, several interviewees told us that the program's interdisciplinary emphasis on "training people to go into applied settings . . . [and] manage water resources" permeated every aspect of its curriculum, from the required inter- and multidisciplinary course work to the culminating out-of-class team project in which students brought their stock of interdisciplinary knowledge to bear on a real-world environmental problem in the region.

We also found that a risk-taking environment is an essential attribute of high-quality programs. Our research suggests that students have far more enriching learning experiences when faculty challenge them to question orthodoxies, explore alternate viewpoints, and experiment with new ideas within "safe" learning contexts that are free from excessive competition, ridicule, or penalty. These risk-taking ventures greatly benefit students, pushing them to develop their potential and to emerge as more self-assured, highly skilled professionals.

Interactive Teaching and Learning. In analyzing the nearly eight hundred interviews from our research effort, we found that high-quality programs are constructed around an interactive model of communication in which faculty, students, administrators, staff and, occasionally, alumni and employers, actively participate in and contribute to one another's learning. More specifically, faculty and administrators in quality programs place heavy emphasis on the following attributes: critical dialogue; integrative, hands-on learning; faculty-student mentoring; cooperative peer learning; and out-of-class learning. Since most people have an intuitive understanding of the latter three attributes, we limit our discussion to critical dialogue and integrative learning here.

Many interviewees indicated that critical dialogue is a distinctive feature of high-quality programs. Grounded in the Latin definition of the term *dialogos,* faculty in high-quality programs constantly encourage students to become active participants in the learning process, inviting them to engage in disciplined and mutually enriching dialogues in which they constantly question one another, examine assumptions and alternate points of view, and generate critically informed understandings of knowledge and professional practice. Such challenging and stimulating conversations enrich students' overall learning experiences by giving them opportunities to think critically, to analyze knowledge and practice from multiple perspectives, and to develop new ideas in collaboration with others.

Our research also shows that integrative learning is an important attribute of high-quality programs. As we define it, integrative learning refers to the bringing together of two or more parts to form a whole, such as theory with practice, self with subject, or learning with living. In high-quality programs, faculty actively seek to connect what students are learning in their classes to tangible situations in the outside world through a variety of activities: some give lectures in which they draw on real-world issues to provide more than textbook presentations of theories in their fields; others use hands-on activities such as case studies, role plays, artistic performances, field research, and laboratory experiments to challenge students to link theory with practice. Not surprisingly, integrative learning activities greatly benefit students, giving them valuable opportunities, as one business student told us, "to work the concepts through in real life. Instead of just sitting there and cramming a lot of book knowledge into your head, I could apply what I was learning. . . . I really felt like I was bumped up to another level of education, to another level of thinking."

Connected Program Requirements. People in high-quality programs also invest heavily in a fourth cluster of attributes: connected program requirements. Time and again, we observed that faculty and administrators in these programs design curricular requirements that challenge students to bridge the worlds of theory and practice—as well as the classroom and workplace—through the following sequential learning experiences: *planned breadth and depth course work, a professional residency,* and *a tangible product.* We briefly comment on these three attributes here.

Contrary to what the literature on program quality suggests, simply requiring students to complete a blend of core and specialized course work does not necessarily enhance the quality of a graduate program. Rather, evidence from our study shows that students have higher-quality learning experiences when faculty and administrators regularly discuss and evaluate the knowledge, skills, and practices they expect students to learn and then craft a coherent set of required core and specialized course work in light of them. Such a carefully planned and integrated mix of generalized and specialized course work helps students to form both broad and deep understandings of knowledge that, in turn, enhances their professional competencies and improves their workplace effectiveness.

A professional residency—an internship, practicum, research or teaching assistantship—is also a vital component of high-quality programs. Students have more enriching learning experiences when faculty challenge them to apply and test what they have learned in their classes to concrete problems in the real world. Intensive, hands-on learning experiences are often valuable for students, enabling them to make creative and useful connections between theory and practice, to hone and gain confidence in their professional skills, and to strengthen their professional identities.

Our research similarly indicates that a tangible product is a key attribute of high-quality programs. Whether a thesis, project report, or artistic performance, this culminating program requirement provides students with an important opportunity to demonstrate to themselves and others that they have mastered the necessary knowledge, skills, and practices to contribute meaningfully to their chosen fields of study. We cannot overemphasize the benefits of this attribute for enhancing student learning. Time and again faculty, administrators, students, alumni, and employers told us that in completing a tangible product, students improved their analytical and written communication skills, became more holistic, "big picture" thinkers, and developed into more independent, self-assured professionals.

Adequate Resources. Finally, in analyzing interviews and various written documents from our forty-seven program sample, we identified adequate resources as the last cluster of attributes in our engagement theory of quality. Our review of the evidence indicates that when program administrators, faculty, and institutional administrators are committed to developing and sustaining programs of high quality, they devote substantial time and effort to securing monetary and nonmonetary support for students, faculty, and basic infrastructure. More specifically, we discovered that certain types of resource support—whether monetary, such as in support for basic infrastructure needs, or nonmonetary, such as in supportive faculty promotion and merit policies—can do much to facilitate and enhance faculty and student engagement in the teaching and learning process.

These five clusters of attributes form our engagement theory of quality. From our perspective, the theory provides faculty, administrators, and others with a new vantage point for understanding and assessing program quality in graduate education in at least three ways.

First, and perhaps most important, since the theory is premised on an emerging definition of quality—one that places student learning squarely at its center—it challenges faculty and administrators to reconsider how they define and assess quality in their own programs. In other words, it provides stakeholders involved with program development and evaluation responsibilities with an alternate perspective on program quality that stresses the centrality of student learning in quality assessment efforts.

Second, anchored in a large body of empirical research, the theory provides supporting explanations as to how and why specific program attributes enhance students' learning. As noted earlier, not one current view of quality systematically explores or documents linkages between program attributes, student learning experiences, and student learning outcomes. It is, therefore, not surprising that faculty, administrators, and institutional researchers seldom assess how various program attributes—such as a thesis or well-stocked library—enhance or diminish the quality of students' learning experiences, let alone examine their effects on student learning outcomes. Our research, in contrast, not only provides an inclusive view of how various program attributes affect student learning, but it also offers accompanying explanations as to why these attributes really matter to the quality of a program. As such, we believe that the theory has the potential to provide faculty, administrators, and institutional researchers with a more comprehensive perspective on what program quality "is" and how they might go about assessing it in terms of student learning.[2] Like every theory, however, ours is not immune from further testing, and we strongly encourage institutional researchers to test the theoretical linkages we have documented.

Third, the theory identifies a number of both reconceptualized and entirely new attributes that have not been previously discussed in the program quality literature. In particular, our research led us to rethink our traditional understandings of faculty, students, and resources by reconceptualizing them in terms of diversity, engagement, and support for teaching and learning. In addition, we identified many new attributes of quality in our study, including engaged leadership, a risk-taking environment, and critical dialogue. These attributes—and the theory that informs them—suggest a new set of quality standards and indicators by which faculty, administrators, and institutional researchers can assess and judge the quality of graduate and professional programs.[3]

A few examples at this juncture may be instructive. For instance, what criteria and indicators might we suggest for our newly reconceptualized view of students? As we noted earlier, student quality has traditionally been assessed largely in terms of academic ability and the quality of effort that students have invested in their studies. Reconceptualizing student quality in terms of diversity and engagement, however, yields a set of new quality criteria (or standards) and indicators, several of which are not easily quantifiable (see Table 4.2). As we see it, a key challenge for institutional researchers is to refine the indicators that we have developed for each attribute in our theory and to construct appropriate instruments that will assist future efforts to assess program quality.

We invite faculty, administrators, and institutional researchers to use our theory as a thinking device for understanding and assessing quality in their programs. Consonant with these ends, we strongly advocate a view of quality assessment that is ongoing in nature and stresses the use of assessment findings for program improvement. In particular, various course-embedded and annual performance review assessment methods—including student and faculty portfolio assessment, classroom research, student and peer evaluations of teaching, and focus group interviews with members of standing advisory councils and alumni groups—have the potential to yield the kinds of useful data that will help faculty, administrators, and institutional researchers to document and better understand the quality of their own graduate and professional programs.

**Table 4.2. Criteria and Indicators for the Attribute
"Diverse and Engaged Students"**

Criterion	Indicators
Student Diversity	Students with a variety of educational, life, and professional workplace experiences are represented in the program.
	Male and female students from a variety of racial, ethnic, and socioeconomic backgrounds are represented.
Engagement in Teaching and Learning	Students actively contribute diverse perspectives on knowledge and practice to class discussions.
	Students demonstrate a visible commitment to their own and others' learning (via their participation in classroom discussions, cooperative learning activities, individual and group projects, independent studies, and research).
Departmental Policies and Practices	Departmental student admissions policies emphasize a variety of criteria, including educational background, life experience, professional nonuniversity workplace experience, cultural diversity, academic achievement, and motivation for learning.
	Admissions decisions are based heavily on the "goodness of fit" between student goals and those of faculty and the program.

Source: Haworth and Conrad, 1997, p. 180. Used by permission of Allyn & Bacon.

Conclusion

In this chapter, we have considered various views of quality, noted their short-comings, and advanced a new view that stresses the importance of learners and learning in defining and assessing graduate program quality. In so doing, we have outlined a theory of program quality—the first of its kind in the litera-ture—that describes what a high-quality program might look like if it were constructed around a learning-centered view of quality. Further, we have briefly suggested how faculty, administrators, and institutional researchers might use the theory and its attributes to think about, document, and assess quality in their own programs.

We conclude with a personal anecdote that, at least in our minds, sug-gests that our learning-centered view of quality and engagement theory may be on the right track. At the beginning of this past academic year, Jennifer had a conversation with her older brother, Tim, who shared with her an amusing story about his six-year-old daughter, Katie. As Tim told Jennifer, it was the night before Katie's first day of school. As he was tucking her in bed, she cupped her hand, held it to her father's ear, and said in a whisper, "Daddy, I have a secret. I'll tell you what it is, but you can't tell anyone else." My brother agreed (so much for secrets), and Katie said with an expectant enthusiasm in her voice, "Daddy, tomorrow when I go to school, I'm gonna do that learning thing."

Whether learned from a six-year-old or from hundreds of adults in a national research study, the message is clear: learners and learning are what schools, colleges, and universities are all about. As our research indicates, faculty and administrators in high-quality graduate programs understand this and, like Jennifer's niece, take that "learning thing" seriously. They nurture program cultures and pedagogical, curricular, and assessment practices designed to enrich student learning. They make student learning—and its continuous improvement—the organizing principle around which decisions related to teaching, assessment, resource allocation, and human resources revolve. And they recognize the pivotal role that engaged participants play in making high-quality student learning happen on a daily basis.

Notes

1. Terenzini and Pascarella based their conclusion on a systematic examination of nearly 2,600 studies on undergraduate education and its effects on student learning and development. While we recognize that their work concentrated on undergraduate education and program quality, our examination of program quality in forty-seven master's programs across the country corroborates their conclusion. This should not be a surprise, since the vast majority of conventional attributes of quality were originally identified in examinations of doctoral program quality.

2. In *Emblems of Quality in Higher Education* (Haworth and Conrad, 1997), we outline a comprehensive framework for assessing and improving the quality of academic programs. Grounded in our theory of quality, the framework is composed of a set of guiding principles, questions to inform assessment and improvement, and quality assessment criteria and indicators.

3. A detailed discussion of various standards and indicators for each of the attributes in our theory can be found in Chapter Nine of Haworth and Conrad (1997).

JENNIFER GRANT HAWORTH *is assistant professor of higher education at Loyola University Chicago.*

CLIFTON F. CONRAD *is professor of higher education at the University of Wisconsin-Madison.*

An institutional perspective on doctoral student attrition is provided,
demonstrating how Berkeley's graduate school went about investigating
doctoral student attrition in order to increase student retention.

Increasing Student Retention in Graduate and Professional Programs

Maresi Nerad, Debra Sands Miller

Increasingly, state legislators request quantifiable measurement of the outcome of advanced-degree programs, particularly doctoral programs. For example, in 1989 the California state senate, in response to concerns about lengthening time to the doctoral degree in the face of the need to diversify faculty and the projected shortage of doctorates, required the University of California to undertake a study of time-to-degree. In 1990, concern about high rates of doctoral student attrition and the subsequent assumptions about the inefficiency of universities resulted in Senate Concurrent Resolution 103, which mandated a study of doctoral completion rates.

Currently, educational policymakers in several states want assessments of doctoral education and professional outcomes to include measurements relative to the graduate's subsequent career path. So far, however, no methodology has been developed for doing this in a meaningful way.[1] While universities can usefully monitor time-to-degree and completion rates and be aware of any trends, focusing on such quantifiable measures alone neglects an essential and unquantifiable outcome of graduate education: the formation of a cultured mind. This valuable outcome can occur, regardless of whether the doctoral program has been completed or employment found in the specific field in which the degree was completed.

Although the current political movement toward greater public accountability through measurable outcomes has gained momentum in recent years,

The authors would like to thank Betty Liu of the Graduate Division's Information and Technology Unit for producing the data for this study and Judi Sui for overseeing data production and for advising us on its use. Thanks also to Dean Joseph Cerny for his careful reading and comments.

graduate deans have always been concerned about the outcomes of graduate and professional education and the numbers of students who successfully complete a degree program. Since the founding of the Association of American Universities in 1900, graduate deans, in studying graduate student attrition, have decried the waste of student energy, hope, and money on the one hand, and the dissipation of faculty time and effort on the other (Slate, 1994; Berelson, 1960). Not surprisingly, policymakers have focused and continue to focus on the institutional costs when student attrition rates are high. Specifically, in times of reduced government spending for public programs, universities become targets for potential savings measures. Under this intense public scrutiny, policymakers view high attrition rates as an obvious sign of waste and inefficiency. As the argument goes, not only are individual faculty affected (Lunnebord and Lunnebord, 1973, Tucker, Gottlieb, and Pease, 1964), but also resources are wasted at the departmental (Cook and Swanson, 1978; Long, 1987) and institutional levels (Tucker, Gottlieb, and Pease, 1964). There are also significant social costs: the loss of productivity from fine minds (Gillingham, Seneca, and Taussig, 1991) and shortages of scientists and professionals during periods of peak labor market demand (Benkin, 1984).

Graduate schools that are in charge of collecting and maintaining graduate student data are in a unique position to monitor the effectiveness of the graduate education process, the quality of their graduate programs, and the outcomes of graduate study. In institutions where graduate schools do not have an institutional research capacity, they may want to work closely with the institutional research office. Collaborating with such a unit, a graduate school can systematically analyze students' completion and attrition rates and use these figures as indicators of possible strengths or weaknesses in their programs. However, they also need to probe deeper into the issues that influence graduate student attrition, undertaking qualitative investigations that allow for an understanding of *why* students leave before completing the desired degree. Only then will institutions be able to design and implement effective policies and activities to improve program quality and, as a result, retain more students.

Using the example of the University of California, Berkeley, in this chapter, we provide an institutional perspective on doctoral student attrition, demonstrating how Berkeley's graduate school went about investigating doctoral student attrition with an eye toward increasing student retention. We discuss the methods we used, our findings, our conclusions, and the activities we implemented to improve completion rates.

We seek to add to the developing body of literature on graduate student attrition that combines both quantitative and qualitative data and that includes the perspectives of both parties involved in the attrition process—doctoral students and departmental faculty and staff (Golde, 1994; Jacks, Chubin, Porter, and Connolly, 1983; Lovitts, 1996; Nerad, 1991; Nerad and Cerny, 1993; Nerad and Stewart, 1991). In the following sections, we demonstrate how research can inform policies and strategies for increasing graduate student retention by focus-

Figure 5.1. Increasing Graduate Student Retention

Research ⟶ Results ⟶ **Recommendations**
Activities Implemented

Quantitative Data analysis	*Early Leavers* No Ph.D. intended	*Institutional Policies and Strategies*	*Working with Departments*	*Working with Students*
Qualitative Interviews	Field switches Institution switches Mismatch Frustrated expectations Student professionals	Monitoring progress First-year evaluation Annual report on progress in candidacy Financial support structure	Faculty advising and mentoring Departmental staff Support Activity guides	Orientation program Grant proposal writing workshops Dissertation writing workshops Interdisciplinary research retreats
	Late Leavers Undecided students Adviser-student relationship Lack of financial support Departmental climate			Abstracts of UCB dissertations-in-progress Publications Job search assistance

Source: Nerad and Cerny, 1991, p. 5. Used by permission of the Council of Graduate Schools.

ing on the interplay of institutional, disciplinary, and student characteristics (see Figure 5.1).

Data Analysis

Our first step in studying doctoral student attrition was to analyze the available data on doctoral students' progress. In the late 1960s, the Graduate Division (the graduate school at Berkeley) established a longitudinal, computerized database, which we jokingly refer to as our monster file. This database stores the registration and degrees record for every graduate student ever enrolled at U.C. Berkeley since 1962. Thus, we possessed the capacity to examine completion rates of our master's and doctoral students over more than three decades.

Our database identifies completion rates by each entering cohort over a twelve-year period (allowing twelve years ensures that the vast majority of students had time to complete the degree). The database report contains five columns: column one indicates the number of elapsed years in the degree program (years one through twelve); column two shows the number of students starting the doctoral program in a particular department; column three (pending) indicates that the student is either registered or has advanced to candidacy but has not yet completed the degree, or is not registered and advanced to candidacy; column four shows the number of degrees awarded; and column five shows whether the student has left.

We assess graduate student attrition in two ways. Before advancement to candidacy, a student is recorded as having left when she or he has not been registered for two consecutive years. Thus, column five will always be zero in years one and two. After advancement to candidacy, a student is regarded as having "left without a degree" only when the Graduate Division receives official notification of lapsed candidacy from the student's graduate program.

In order to obtain current information on students' status, the Graduate Division sends out to each department a list of names of students who should have completed the degree according to the department's established time-to-degree goals. The department is responsible for contacting each student to find out whether the student has made a definite decision to leave the program without completing, or if he or she still plans to work toward the degree. Once the department has verified each student's status, it notifies the Graduate Division. As soon as the Graduate Division receives information that a student is either still working on the dissertation or has left the graduate program, the information is entered into the database, and his or her status is classified as either "pending" or "dropped." In this way, the Graduate Division maintains accurate, up-to-date records on each student.

We began continuously analyzing student cohorts with the cohort that entered in 1975. We grouped three annual cohorts together in order to provide a larger number of cases for analysis and then followed this over time, thereby analyzing the 1975–1977, 1978–1980, and 1981–1983 cohorts.

Data Analysis Results. In general, we found that about 80 percent of all self-designated doctoral students completed a graduate program, but not all who indicated the doctorate as their degree goal on their application actually completed the degree. That is, some graduated with a master's degree. Thus, the doctoral degree completion rate is lower than the overall graduate degree completion rate. For the 1981–1983 cohort, we found that of the 78 percent who had completed a graduate program after eleven years of study, 18 percent had received master's degrees, and 60 percent had received doctorates. Seventeen percent left without a degree, and 5 percent were still "pending" (in the latter group, approximately half completed their degree after year eleven).

Fields of Study. We discerned that doctoral completion rates varied widely across major fields of study. For the 1981–1983 cohort, students in the biological and physical sciences had the highest completion rate (73 percent), followed by engineering (66 percent), the social sciences (53 percent), the professional schools (48 percent), and finally, the humanities (44 percent).

We also found that a low completion rate correlated with long time-to-degree. Although we did not compare the same cohort, we found that for students who completed their doctoral degrees between 1990 and 1994, the average campus time-to-doctoral degree was 7.1 years; the median time was 6.3

years. Physical sciences, engineering, and biological sciences had the shortest time-to-degree (median time: engineering, 5.3 years; physical and biological sciences, 5.7 years). The social sciences, professional schools,[2] and humanities had the longest time-to-degree (median time: social sciences and professional schools, 7.3 years; humanities, 8.6 years).

Men and Women. Our analysis likewise showed variations by gender, with a smaller proportion of women than men receiving a degree. For the 1975– 1977 cohort, for example, 44 percent of all women and 51 percent of all men completed the doctorate; in the 1981–1983 cohort, these percentages rose to 52 percent and 65 percent, respectively. This pattern was consistent across fields for all analyzed cohorts, prompting us to conduct individual interviews and focus groups with students in order to find explanations for this consistent difference.

Citizenship and Race-Ethnicity. In addition to variations by gender, there were variations by citizenship status and race-ethnicity. International students, both men and women, consistently had the highest completion rates in all fields and in all cohorts. We also found that non-Asian minority students were less likely than Caucasian students to complete and that this difference was statistically significant. In spite of these discrepancies, we noticed that completion rates for non-Asian minority students increased in the three consecutive cohorts from a low of 40 percent in the first cohort to 50 percent and 54 percent for the second and third cohorts. We are still trying to understand the complex reasons behind these differential completion rates. In an earlier article (Nerad and Cerny, 1993), we began to develop explanations for field-specific factors contributing to differential completion rates.

When Do Students Leave? In order to understand more fully the reasons for attrition and to develop policies and programs to retain more students, we wanted to know when students were most likely to withdraw from doctoral study. Our research reveals a clear pattern: students are far more likely to leave before advancement to candidacy (between years one and three of the doctoral program) than after. Using the 1981–1983 cohort as an illustration, of the total enrollment, fully one-quarter left between years one and three (we refer to these students as "early leavers"), whereas only 10 percent left between years four and eleven (we refer to these students as "late leavers"). After eleven years, 5 percent were still pending. Our data confirm the findings of Benkin's 1984 dissertation and further disproved the common folklore that the majority of those leaving without a Ph.D. are ABDs—students who have completed doctoral requirements, "all but the dissertation."

Time of Attrition by Field. We also found a high degree of variation in the time of attrition across fields. For the 1981–1983 cohort, the biological sciences and physical sciences both had a lower percentage of earlier leavers (20 percent), as well as a lower percentage of late leavers (6 percent). The professional schools, the arts, and languages and literature had the highest proportions of early leavers (31, 33, and 29 percent, respectively) and the highest proportions of late leavers (14, 19, and 15 percent, respectively). In the social sciences, 26 percent left early and 13 percent left late, whereas in engineering early leavers (25 percent) far outpaced late leavers (7 percent).

Women's attrition patterns differ from men's in the early leaver category in the biological sciences, physical sciences, engineering, and social sciences (a 7 percent higher attrition rate during the first three years). Women and men have very similar attrition patterns in the humanities and professional schools.

Given these results, we began to search for explanations for these figures. Our first step was to inform our departments about these findings and to solicit explanations for attrition rates and proposals for improving retention of their doctoral students.

Department Responses. At Berkeley, the Graduate Division sends out a statistical report triennially on the completion rates and time-to-degree of each department's students to the department chair. In an accompanying letter, the dean requests a reply specifying what the department will do to improve its completion rates. Aside from collecting the responses to this letter, we have not systematically surveyed departments. But their explanations, in addition to our informal conversations with faculty, typically yield the standard responses discussed below.[3] (We are aware that a more systematic collection of data is also necessary.)

Some departments, for instance, point out that the high attrition rates recorded in years one through three are a statistical artifact. These departments claim that students, particularly women, apply for the doctorate when they fully intend to graduate with a master's degree, often doing so because their program of choice does not admit students for a terminal master's degree. In addition, they say, students are aware that departments offer financial support for doctoral students but rarely for master's students. Therefore, students apply for the doctorate, even though their goal is the master's degree. Since it is impossible for institutions to account for such strategies, the apparent early attrition may be higher than the "actual" Ph.D. attrition rates would be without such students.

Other departments attribute attrition to insufficient financial support for graduate students. Still others suggest that retention rates would improve if students took more initiative and did not expect "handholding" from faculty. Certainly, some departments acknowledge that they need to improve retention rates; unfortunately, most hope to do this by improving the admissions process only. They assert that if faculty and students' interests are better matched, a higher retention rate will result.[4]

With few exceptions, these responses indicate that graduate faculty and chairs at Berkeley view attrition primarily as a result of external forces and not as a consequence of the structure of the program or departmental practices. These responses are consistent with the assumptions that underpin much of the previous research on doctoral attrition (Golde, 1995) and reflect the need to include in a renewed discussion of graduate student attrition the role of institutional barriers to student success and the processes by which organizational or individual factors interact, as well as the voices of the students themselves (Golde, 1994; Nerad, 1991).

Qualitative Research

Research on undergraduate attrition has shown that explaining attrition involves both identifying who is most likely to leave and the conditions that exacerbate attrition (Golde, 1995; Tinto, 1993). Even though at Berkeley, we had comprehensive statistical information on how many students left, who they were, and when they left, we did not have an in-depth understanding of the reasons why students left their programs, let alone the factors that influenced their decisions to leave. Consequently, we added a qualitative component to our quantitative research on doctoral student attrition to fill this void.

Conducting qualitative research on attrition poses a unique problem for an institution, that is, locating individuals who have left or who are considering leaving. When students are considering leaving, they seldom voice their intentions. By the time the institution or graduate school knows that students are gone, a great deal of time may have elapsed, and current address or telephone information may be unavailable. At U.C. Berkeley, we surmounted this problem in several ways.

First, in order to identify students who were at risk of leaving, we sent a letter to all campus graduate assistants—the departmental staff in charge of graduate student affairs—and asked them to provide us with the names of students who they knew were seriously considering leaving or who had recently left the doctoral program. Using these lists, we called students and arranged interviews. Not only were we able to contact students identified for us by the staff, but the interviews themselves had a snowball effect—an interview with one student inevitably generated names of other students who were seriously considering leaving. In some cases, an interviewed student encouraged others to be interviewed also. Students with strong reasons for leaving often knew others in similar situations and felt strongly that all students' stories needed to be heard.

We conducted individual, in-depth, semistructured interviews. During the interviews, we walked students through the five major stages of doctoral study: course work, preparation for the oral qualifying exam, finding a dissertation topic, dissertation research and writing, and applying for professional employment (Nerad, 1991). Interviews revolved around a number of questions, including the following: Why did you choose to attend graduate school? At the time you started graduate study, did you have an idea of how long it took, on average, to complete a doctorate in your field? Do you regret the time you spent in graduate school or count it as wasted time? If you could do it over again, what would you do differently? Additional questions focused on assessing how institutional factors such as financial support or the presence or absence of a departmental program structure, as well as individual factors such as being a student parent, re-entry student, or full-time working professional while in graduate school, affected students and their decision to discontinue doctoral study.

Interviews were tape-recorded and transcribed with the student's permission, while safe-guarding anonymity and confidentiality. To our surprise, students were, after initial cautiousness, very willing to talk. In most cases, students candidly reflected on their situation and, surprisingly, all welcomed the opportunity to have someone with official university status listen to their stories. Most went away from the interview feeling that the institution was concerned about and interested in their fate.

Results of the Interviews. Strictly speaking, a doctoral degree program consists of four distinct stages: taking courses, preparing for and taking the qualifying examination, finding a dissertation topic and adviser and writing a dissertation prospectus, and undertaking research and writing the dissertation. For our purposes, however, a fifth stage—applying for a professional position— has been added. The majority of students look for jobs while still in graduate school, and faculty and students agreed that the absence or presence of a job offer had an impact on the ability to persist and complete the degree (Nerad, 1991). Within these stages, a natural division between early and late leavers occurs between stages two and three; that is, before a student is advanced to candidacy for the Ph.D. Contrary to popular belief, we found that the majority of the graduate students who failed to earn their doctorates left the program early, before advancement to candidacy. We, therefore, report attrition factors as they pertain to early and late leavers.

Early Leavers. Early leavers fall into several categories: those who never intended to get a doctorate, field switchers, institution switchers, students whose interests did not match those of faculty, those frustrated with the degree program, and students who have professional careers outside the university. Each is discussed in turn.[5] In the majority of cases, several factors combined over time that influenced students' decision to leave. For analytical purposes, however, we describe each factor separately.

No Ph.D. Intended. There are groups of students who appear statistically in doctoral attrition statistics but whose original intent was to earn a master's degree. Some enrolled as Ph.D. students in departments with discrete master's programs in order to obtain financial support.

Field Switchers. We labeled a second group of students who appear statistically as early leavers as "field switchers." These students, who transferred from one doctoral program to another or from a doctoral program to a professional degree program within the institution, appear in the attrition statistics as not having completed their original degree program, though they may have completed in another. For example, a number of students of color at Berkeley left doctoral programs in the sciences or social sciences to attend law school. When questioned about their motivations, students often offered a variation on this response: "As a first-generation college goer, I feel I can give more to my community by earning a law degree than by earning a Ph.D." In general, these students were politically aware, action-oriented individuals for whom a shorter duration of study and a more structured program with a clear professional path proved more attractive than a research degree and a tentative academic appointment with its accompanying tenure hurdle.

Institution Switchers. Some students who are included in Berkeley's attrition statistics transferred to another institution and may have completed their doctorates elsewhere. Transfers occur for a variety of reasons—for example, when faculty advisers relocate or when students learn that the specific research emphasis they sought is not offered at Berkeley.

We lack the means of linking our data with data from other institutions, so we do not know the incidence of transfer and completion. Data from the annual Survey of Earned Doctorates may permit such an analysis in the future. Other research, including a study at U.C. San Diego (Morton, 1976), suggests that excluding transfer students who successfully complete master's or doctoral degrees elsewhere from attrition statistics could lower an institution's noncompletion rate by 8 to 10 percentage points.

Mismatch. Some students left early when they discovered a mismatch between their interests and those of the program. Although Berkeley's admissions process is very comprehensive, some students may not have carefully researched the program. We found that these students occasionally accepted an offer of admission based on the institution's reputation or on outdated catalogues. Many told us they had not taken the time to determine which faculty were currently in the department, nor had they familiarized themselves with the faculty's research agendas. Sometimes, students expected a particular focus to be represented among faculty in the department and were disappointed to find no specialist in their area of interest when they arrived. Over the course of time, these students left, either because they did not want to change their focus or because when they did change their focus to comply with a faculty suggestion, their interest was superficial, and it could not sustain them to completion.

Frustrated Expectations. Another group of students left their doctoral programs because graduate student life did not meet their original expectations. Many such students found the large institutional setting alienating. Others came only to study with "the famous Nobel laureate" but were frustrated by the brevity of the appointment and the lack of interest this person displayed in them or their work and lost interest in their studies entirely. Last, several students indicated that they discontinued their doctoral studies because they did not have the "calling" to do research. These students often began doctoral work with an idealistic vision of research, but when faced with its nitty-gritty, everyday realities, they grew increasingly disillusioned and left.

Student Professionals. Students in the professional schools frequently left doctoral study for specific reasons. These students, most of whom held responsible jobs and saw the doctoral program as a means toward further professional advancement, often had a difficult time with certain aspects of academic culture. Some struggled with program requirements or an academic structure in which they were not always accorded the professional respect or recognition to which they were accustomed. Others recognized that their career goals were, in fact, incompatible with academic life. One student in forestry who wanted to complete the doctorate in order to move up in the national forestry administration, for example, was appalled that his professor "never got out into the forest."

Late Leavers. We classified students who left their doctoral programs late into the following categories: those who were undecided about the goal of their studies, those whose relationship with their adviser went sour, those who lacked adequate financial support, and those who were discouraged by a chilly departmental climate.

The Undecided Student. The third and fourth years of doctoral study are especially demanding for students in the humanities, social sciences, and professional schools. During this time, students must decide on a dissertation topic, choose an adviser, write the dissertation prospectus, and begin their research. Students who lack a clear academic focus struggle at this time, and some drop out. As we learned in our interviews, these students have a difficult time choosing a dissertation topic, forsaking their multiple interests and narrowing down to one. These students often had no clear professional goal in mind, which made it cumbersome for them to select a topic and stay focused on the dissertation as a means to an end: developing the ability to perform and complete a research project. Thinking they had to explain the whole world in their dissertation, they floundered and withdrew when faced with departmental pressures to present a proposal.

Adviser-Student Relationship. Poor adviser-student relationships also contribute to students' decision to abandon doctoral study. In the realm of spoiled adviser-student relationships, we found precipitating incidents ranging from overuse of skilled students as technical assistants and cheap labor in the laboratories, to cases where students unconsciously projected a parent-child relationship onto the adviser-student relationship and then rebelled against the adviser. In these cases, students—recognizing their dependency on faculty for a future letter of recommendation and professional contacts—often became overly cautious about candidly discussing the relationship with their adviser. Such behavior often led to misunderstandings and unarticulated expectations between advisers and students, often resulting in a termination of the relationship.

Lack of Financial Support. Our research indicates that a lack of financial support is also a major factor in late attrition. In the humanities, mathematics, professional schools, and social sciences, we spoke with several students who lamented the lack of funding for dissertation research. Many of the students had already taught as Graduate Student Instructors (GSIs or teaching assistants) for the maximum number of allowable years and could not secure further sources of academic funding.[6] This lack of financial support—particularly if exacerbated by a poor advising relationship or a bleak job market—contributed to these students' decision to discontinue doctoral study.

In the biological sciences, engineering, and physical sciences, we encountered other scenarios. Here, students emphasized the precarious nature of doctoral study in their disciplines. A few, for instance, noted how their dissertation research had been suspended when their advisers ran out of research funding.

Others lamented the lack of GSI positions due to low undergraduate enrollments in these fields. Once again, limited financial support, particularly if coupled with a distant and uncooperative adviser-student relationship, prompted many of these students to leave without a degree.

Departmental Climate. Departmental climate, or the general atmosphere and environment present in a department, stood out in our interviews as a final, potent factor coloring students' perceptions of the doctoral experience. Time and again, students told us that a "chilly" departmental climate—one in which students had the impression that they were wasting the time of the faculty or encountered few expressions of concern about their personal and professional advancement—often exacerbated other difficulties (such as a lack of funding or personal problems) and contributed to their decision to withdraw from the university.

A chilly departmental climate was one especially salient attrition factor for women. In our interviews, women repeatedly stressed the importance of receiving personalized attention and feedback from faculty in order for students to have continued faith in their own capabilities. To be sure, we also spoke with male students who were angry about the absence of faculty feedback on their work. In general, however, this factor seldom led men to question their intellectual capabilities or their capacity to do research, and only occasionally affected their progress toward completion of the doctorate (Nerad, 1992).

We do not claim to have exhausted the number of possible factors leading to attrition; rather we have sought to describe the most common. In all cases, we found that the interplay of the student's specific personal characteristics with circumstantial or structural events in the program caused a student to withdraw.

Recommendations for Increasing Student Retention

Combining the results from quantitative and qualitative research, the Graduate Division developed recommendations and designed and implemented activities to lower attrition rates. Since attrition is not based on an isolated phenomenon but on the interplay of institutional and student characteristics, the Graduate Division adopted a three-pronged approach to improving doctoral student retention at Berkeley.

First Prong: Institutional Policies and Strategies. The Graduate Division has four principal policies and strategies that apply to all graduate programs.

Monitoring Progress. Graduate schools must systematically monitor completion rates and the progress of graduate students throughout their graduate careers and regularly report its findings to departments. Berkeley's triennial report to departments and requested response was described above. Where we think change is necessary, the dean conducts a half-day visit in which he or she talks to students and faculty, presents current data demonstrating improvement or nonimprovement, and requests a justification if no improvement is indicated.

First-Year Evaluation. We recommend that departments conduct a first-year evaluation, during which a team of faculty meets separately with each student to discuss the student's progress and to evaluate whether the student's expectations about the program and the content of its offerings are being met. If there is a mismatch between expectations and the department's program, departments are encouraged to point out that students have other options within Berkeley or at other universities with which Berkeley has a reciprocal enrollment agreement. Transferring is also considered as a viable and nonpejorative option.

Annual Report on Progress in Candidacy. We developed an "Annual Review of Doctoral Candidates" to encourage regular faculty advising and mentoring in all programs when course taking ceases after advancement to candidacy. Annual meetings with at least two dissertation committee members are intended to give each student a chance to discuss last year's progress, to map out next year's work, and to receive feedback on progress and advice on further research from two committee members at the same time. The policy requires that each department send a copy of the "Annual Report on Progress in Candidacy in the Doctoral Program" form to the Graduate Division. This form is completed by the student, committee members, and chair of the dissertation committee. Students initially perceived this review as just another hurdle, but they came to realize that it offers a valuable opportunity to identify problems and resources and to help keep them on track. The written record is useful to them, as well as to the department.

Financial Support Structure. At two critical stages in the doctoral degree program, students should be freed, if possible, from teaching or working in an area unrelated to their research: when they are preparing for the qualifying exam and developing the dissertation proposal, and when they are compiling their research findings and writing the dissertation. We encourage departments not to allocate all their funds for fellowships to attract new students to the institution, but to reserve a portion for students at later stages of the degree program. The Graduate Division has also allocated funds for a number of dissertation year fellowships.

Second Prong: Working with Departments. The following initiatives have been introduced at the departmental level to decrease time-to-degree and lower attrition.

Advising and Mentoring. At Berkeley, we operate on the belief that faculty mentoring and advising are key components in a successful graduate program, but we distinguish between the two. An adviser is responsible for assisting students in selecting programs of study and for making sure that students make adequate progress toward the degree and fulfill all university requirements. In contrast, a mentor (as defined in the literature [Hall and Sandler, 1983]) is a person who helps the protégé set goals and standards and develop skills; protects the protégé from others to allow room for risk and failure; facilitates a successful entrance into academic and professional circles; and ultimately passes on his or her work to the protégé. Like friendship, this kind of mentoring cannot be forced upon students and faculty (Nerad, 1995).

We understand that increasing the faculty's responsibility for advising is not the solution to the problem of student attrition. Accordingly, we have encouraged a departmental advising and mentoring effort in which the faculty play an important, but not exclusive, role. All faculty members advise, but mentoring is the acknowledged responsibility of the entire department. Departmental seminars and workshops, in addition to individual faculty mentors, provide the mentoring that produces the formal and informal knowledge students need to become professionals in their fields (Nerad, 1995).

The Graduate Division provides each faculty graduate adviser with a *Graduate Adviser's Handbook* and meets with them each semester to discuss common concerns and responsibilities. In addition, the Graduate Division invites faculty members, administrators, and students from selected departments to monthly invitational research seminars on graduate education. Discussions about the role of faculty advising constitute a substantial portion of the agenda.

Departmental Staff Support. Departmental staff play a crucial role in student retention. To help cultivate a caring and responsive staff and to keep the lines of communication open, the Graduate Division originated the Graduate Assistant Advisory Group. Two Graduate Division staff members meet monthly with a group of approximately fifteen graduate assistants from a representative variety of campus departments. The group advises the Graduate Division and informs it about what is going on in the departments and with the students, and responds to prospective changes in policy. This group, in turn, reaches out by means of satellite groups to other graduate assistants with information and to solicit their input. We understand that it is not only necessary to inform the staff about our research results and policies but also to encourage them to see their roles as liaison, student advocate, confidante, and social coordinator as crucial to building community and collegiality in the departments.

Easing the Way. From our interviews with students, we acquired valuable information on special departmental activities that supported students at various stages of their doctoral programs. From this information we developed a guide, *Easing the Way for Graduate Students*, which publicizes positive examples of successful departmental activities. The guide is distributed to department chairs, head graduate advisers, graduate assistants, and department student associations.

Third Prong: Working with Students. In an institution as big as Berkeley, students have to take an active role in their own education. The Graduate Division has used its research findings to design and implement programs that encourage students to complete their degrees and educate them to exercise effective educational strategies on their own behalf.

Orientation Programs. The Graduate Division has implemented first-semester graduate student orientations for new students, international graduate students, and GSIs. In these orientations, we encourage students to take time, when they are beginning doctoral study, to clarify their reasons for going to graduate school. We also provide information on the stages of the doctoral program.

Grant Proposal Writing Workshops. When students are unable to obtain funding for research, they can become discouraged and discontinue their studies. To assist student in locating and applying for funding, we offer grant writing workshops and individual grant proposal consultations to graduate students throughout the academic year.

Dissertation Writing Workshops. Since we learned from interviews and statistical analyses that the beginning of the dissertation writing process is a crucial stage during which many students need help, each year we offer twelve day-long dissertation writing workshops. These workshops include tips on time management; where to begin and how to keep going; how to move from research to writing to revising to finishing; practical advice on organizing, outlining, setting practical goals and tasks; and strategies for working effectively with the dissertation adviser.

Interdisciplinary Research Retreats. Building on an earlier model from the Social Science Research Council to counter the isolation commonly experienced among humanities, social sciences, and professional school students and to foster interdisciplinary research, the Graduate Division and International and Area Studies at U.C. Berkeley have developed interdisciplinary dissertation workshops. These three-day, off-campus workshops bring together students who are working on similar themes but who are in different departments and do not know each other. They help break the sense of isolation that so often attends the dissertation writing experience, precipitate the formation of a cross-disciplinary intellectual community that endures beyond the workshop, and provide fresh impetus for completing work that students may have begun to think irrelevant or doomed to failure.

Abstracts of Berkeley Dissertations-in-Progress. Because only a few students can participate in the interdisciplinary research retreats, the Graduate Division, International and Area Studies, and the U.C. Berkeley Library have established a restricted-access World Wide Web database of abstracts of "Dissertations-in-Progress at U.C. Berkeley." The database is intended to enable doctoral students to locate students in other disciplines and schools across the campus working on related topics and to form writing groups.

Publications. As a result of our research, making the graduate education process as transparent as possible has become a leading principle in our efforts to increase student retention. Once a semester, the Graduate Division publishes *The Graduate: A Newsletter for Graduate Students*. Articles in this publication cover topics such as, "The Agenda for First-Year Students," "Gearing up for the Qualifying Exam," and "Moving Toward Professionalism." In addition, the Graduate Division has produced a guide to academic publishing for doctoral students in the humanities and social sciences.

Academic Job Search Assistance. Finally, we continue to support students in their search for professional employment. Students, especially those who have spent a long time pursuing the degree and who may be questioning whether completing the dissertation matters to their subsequent career, find that having a job offer or prospective job provides the ideal impetus to complete. Consequently, we provide a number of job placement workshops and make videotapes of the sessions available to students who are unable to attend. We also encourage departmental staff to consider job placement as a crucial stage in the doctoral process, to tailor general campus job placement workshops to their students' needs, and to organize sessions in which faculty are available to help students prepare for the job market and think about the next step.

Conclusion

Adopting a comprehensive institutional perspective on doctoral student attrition, the Berkeley Graduate Division has used various research activities to address the issue of doctoral student retention with a focus on improvement. Our research, combining quantitative analyses with qualitative methods, has led to a deeper awareness of the complex interaction of personal and organizational factors and the need to include many stakeholders in our efforts to increase graduate student retention at all levels of the institution: the general administration (graduate services), the departments, and the students themselves. Consequently, we have developed an integrative approach to designing recommendations and programmatic activities. We have implemented institutional policies and strategies, encouraged departmental activities that include staff and faculty, and developed programs to support students at crucial stages of doctoral study.

Notes

1. The Graduate Division at Berkeley is currently undertaking a career path study, funded by the Mellon Foundation, of some six thousand Ph.D.'s who received their degrees between 1983 and 1985 from sixty-one U.S. doctoral granting universities.

2. At Berkeley, professional schools include architecture, business administration, city and regional planning, education, environmental health sciences, energy and resources, environmental design, journalism, library science, jurisprudence and social policy, public health, physical education, public policy, social welfare, and vision science. Law (J.D.) and medicine (M.D.) are not included.

3. The University of California at San Diego report similar responses from faculty in their doctoral attrition study (Ribak and Littlefield, 1992).

4. There seemed to be two philosophies applied by departments (with no pattern by disciplines). One, institute a strict admissions procedure and then try to finance all students and be diligent about shepherding them through; and two, admit more students and then, before allowing them to proceed, weed them out after one year, or at the time of the prelims, or after the master's degree by means of the qualifying examination.

5. It is important to note that a statistically insignificant number of students, approximately 6 percent, leave Berkeley because they fail their qualifying exams. Students can repeat the qualifying exam once; a failure on the second attempt results in dismissal from the department.

The infrequency of this occurrence, particularly when coupled with what we learned from our interviews, led us to conclude that no single factor—and rarely the lack of academic competency—influenced students' choice to discontinue doctoral study.

6. Teaching as a GSI at Berkeley is limited to eight regular semesters. By exception, a student may be appointed for up to, but not exceeding, twelve semesters.

MARESI NERAD is director of graduate research in the Graduate Division at the University of California, Berkeley.

DEBRA SANDS MILLER is senior writer in the Graduate Division Research Unit at the University of California, Berkeley, and also works as a freelance writer and editor.

Five categories of student outcomes in graduate and professional education are identified, and a framework for assessing each one is offered. Additionally, various methods for collecting data on student outcomes are described and evaluated.

Documenting Student Outcomes in Graduate and Professional Programs

Leonard L. Baird

The assessment of the influence of advanced-degree programs on their students is a critical, if neglected, issue in higher education for two reasons. First, graduate education is a surprisingly common experience in our society. Millions of people have pursued graduate study, and nearly two million are pursuing advanced degrees. Second, the influence of programs on their students has a long-term impact on some of the most critical positions in our society. Given the importance of the effects of graduate programs on their students, it is surprising that relatively little research has pursued these issues. Rather, the main focus of research has been on the prestige of programs and is usually confined to elite institutions (Baird, 1990; Webster, 1992). Despite this relative lack of research, there is much that can be done to examine the influence of graduate programs on students.

The logic of assessing the impact of graduate programs on students is very similar to that used in undergraduate education (Banta, and Associates, 1993; Kells, 1995). That is, while concentrating on outcomes, we must see them within the context of student characteristics and goals, the institutional setting, and the educational process. Perhaps the clearest generalization in higher education research is that student characteristics and situations at entry to a program are the strongest determinants of student outcomes at departure from the program. This generalization applies with equal force at the graduate and undergraduate level. For example, one would expect different outcomes from a graduate program that enrolls students directly from undergraduate study, supports them with assistantships, and has a large research budget compared to one that enrolls returning adults who can attend only part-time because they have full-time jobs and families and that has little research activity. It is very important to consider what students are like when they begin a program when evaluating what they are like when they graduate. Researchers who examine the outcomes of graduate programs must factor in the enormous variation in the profile of students, both within disciplines and across disciplines. For example, the typical doctoral student in education is twelve years older than the average doctoral student in the physical sciences.

Likewise, the institutional setting needs to be considered. Graduate programs vary greatly in wealth and in the availability of assistantships and other support and research activity, both within disciplines and across disciplines. For example, Baird (1991) found that programs that ranked in the top 15 percent in number of journal publications in mechanical engineering would rank in the bottom 15 percent in chemistry, given the same number of publications. Clearly, the support of and the opportunities provided by programs differ greatly. Of equal importance is the variation in the goals of the programs. As Conrad, Haworth, and Millar (1993) found, the variation in program purposes can be very broad, extending the distinctions among them far beyond the traditional classification of preparing for teaching, research, or professional practice. Thus, programs need to be evaluated in terms of the student outcomes that are relevant to their purposes.

The educational process also needs to be examined. If the purpose of examining student outcomes is to improve the program's standing on those outcomes, it can only be done by also examining the educational process and linking the process to the outcomes. There is ample evidence that the process of graduate education varies in a multitude of ways, even within the programs of approximately equivalent prestige (Anderson, Louis, and Earle, 1994; Clark, Hartnett, and Baird, 1976). Various research projects have developed assessments of these processes, which can be used for program or institutional evaluations.

Defining Outcomes

Because of the variety of program goals, it may seem a bewildering task to define the objectives that can be assessed by outcomes. However, a number of generic objectives and outcomes can be assessed with appropriate tailoring to each program (Borden and Banta, 1994; Gaither, 1995). These outcomes can be assessed by a variety of indicators (Botrill and Borden, 1994) and include the following:

Degree Completion. The attainment of a degree in a timely fashion for a high percentage of an entering group should be a fundamental goal of every program.
Knowledge of the Discipline. The basic underpinning of every graduate program is the transmission of the knowledge and skills to master the discipline.
Preparation for Professional Practice. Although this outcome category has different meanings in different disciplines, even the most theoretical discipline has some aspects of professional practice. This category is particularly relevant in applied fields.

Preparation for Research and Inquiry. Although emphasized more in some programs than others, the great majority of programs include some emphasis on the ability to understand and conduct research or inquiry in a manner consistent with the discipline.

Preparation for Teaching. Again varying by discipline, this outcome category has particular relevance to fields such as the humanities, which prepare students for careers in college teaching.

These categories overlap and certainly are not mutually exclusive. For example, many history programs emphasize both preparation for research and teaching. Many psychology programs emphasize both professional practice and research.

Sources of Information

These five categories of outcomes can be assessed by using information of several types, which vary in purpose and availability. These include:

Institutional Data. Institutional data of record can be obtained fairly easily, and often is already available in a usable form, because it serves other purposes (for example, to meet accreditation or state information requirements). However, at the graduate level, records are sometimes maintained in a haphazard or unsystematic fashion (Isaac, 1993). Another source of information is the institutional reports of such agencies as the National Research Council, which can be used for a variety of institutional studies (Ploskonka, 1993).

Information on the Educational Process. This information is most conveniently obtained from surveys and interviews of current students and faculty, although the retrospective evaluations of graduates and the expert views of visiting evaluation teams could be used.

Information on Outcomes at the Completion of Studies. Information about students' status on outcomes that are important to a program can be most conveniently obtained by exit surveys or interviews, although faculty assessments and external evaluators can be used.

Information on Long-Term Outcomes. For most programs, the success of graduates in their academic, research, or professional careers is paramount. Information on the activities and accomplishments of graduates can be most conveniently obtained from surveys of the graduates themselves, although independent assessments of graduates' performance can be obtained from employers or clients and, in the case of research, from national data sets.

Each of these kinds of information can be obtained by a variety of methods, each of which has advantages and disadvantages (Prus and Johnson, 1994). Issues of validity, cost, obtainability, and flexibility need to be considered. Qualitative methods represent an important source of judgments (Mitler and Bers, 1994).

Table 6.1. A Framework for Assessing the Outcomes of
Graduate and Professional Education

	Type of Information			
Category of Outcomes	Basic Facts from Institutional Records	Information on Processes	Information on Outcomes at Completion	Information on Long-Range Outcomes
Degree Completion	1	2	3	4
Knowledge	5	6	7	8
Preparation for Professional Practice	9	10	11	12
Preparation for Research	13	14	15	16
Preparation for Teaching	17	18	19	20

An Assessment Framework

The categories of outcomes and the types of information just described can be viewed together, as shown in Table 6.1. The following discussion provides some options for specific measures for each cell in the table.

Degree Completion. The following information can be collected to assess degree completion in a graduate or professional program.

Basic Facts (Cell 1). Measures include the percentage of each entering year's students who obtain the degree for the total group and disaggregated by gender, racial group, and age. Another important measure is years-to-degree from entry to program for the total group and disaggregated by gender, racial group, and age.

Processes (Cell 2). Views of current students on the effects of various experiences and policies on their likelihood of obtaining the degree can be very valuable, since actions can be taken that would deal with any problems before they finish or leave their programs. Views of faculty on the factors in degree completion and time-to-degree provide an independent and valuable perspective, since faculty are sometimes knowledgeable about issues that students usually do not consider. This information from students and faculty could be obtained by survey or by interviews, or both.

Outcomes at Completion (Cell 3). Information at the completion (or noncompletion) of the program can be obtained via exit surveys or interviews with students who have completed or left the program. Such information can provide various clues on the importance of various experiences and policies as they relate to attrition and retention. In particular, surveys or interviews with students who complete their degrees on the effects of various experiences and policies on the duration of their studies are particularly useful, since they provide the perspective of those who have experienced the entire program.

Long-Range Outcomes (Cell 4). Long-range perspectives on degree completion and time-to-degree can be based on the same kind of information obtained in Cell 3, but from the perspective of those with greater experiences in an academic or professional career.

Knowledge of the Discipline. The following data can be useful in assessing the level of disciplinary knowledge students achieve in a graduate or professional program.

Basic Facts (Cell 5). Mastery of the knowledge and skills of the discipline can be assessed in a few disciplines by the success of students on professional or licensing examinations, the institutional results of which can be obtained from the testing group. However, assessments of the mastery of knowledge in most disciplines must come from other sources. One type of institutional evaluation that can be examined is pass rates on various qualifying examinations. Any examination of students in a program by faculty outside the department or unit provides a relatively independent evaluation. However, this information may be problematic, since a low pass rate could be interpreted as either being due to a department's high standards or as evidence of the inadequate preparation it provides.

Processes (Cell 6). Information on mastery of knowledge in this area can be obtained fairly conveniently from current students who can be surveyed or interviewed about their sense of progress toward the intellectual competencies that are the focus of the department (Smart and Hagedorn, 1994). A more involved and costly approach would have an evaluation team of faculty in the discipline from other institutions examine the curriculum and assess the knowledge of students. This approach could be fairly cost-effective if it were part of an assessment consortium, as described below.

Outcomes at Completion (Cell 7). Students' knowledge at the completion of studies can be evaluated by a ready source of information about students' mastery of the discipline in the evaluation forms of the external examiners or readers that are required by many graduate schools. Almost all institutions require a nondepartmental reader of dissertations as a representative of the graduate school. These readers are usually asked to provide an evaluation of the quality of the dissertation, the rigor and fairness of the examination, and the performance of the degree candidate. Information from a number of candidates could be summarized for a graduate program and used for evaluation purposes. Further, the standard evaluation forms filled out by the graduate school representative could be rewritten to include specific assessments of the program's preparation of students. Likewise, many institutions assign a graduate school representative at qualifying or "general" examinations. They, too, could be asked to provide evaluations.

Graduating students could be surveyed or interviewed for their mastery of knowledge and skills, as in Cell 6. The views of students who have experienced the entire process are particularly valuable. One innovative method for obtaining this information is to ask all graduating students to write a letter outlining their views of the value of particular courses, the coherence of the curriculum, the success with which the discipline is covered, or any other concerns they have. The instructions for the letter should be fairly open-ended, since the faculty may be blind to weak spots in the program. Another useful, if costly, possibility is to have a panel of experts in the discipline read the most recent dissertations to evaluate the extent to which they indicate mastery of the discipline.

Long-Range Outcomes (Cell 8). The long-range impact of a program on the knowledge and skills of its graduates is one of the most important outcomes. One of the most useful sources of information about the impact of programs on their students comes from the views of recent graduates. Graduates who are pursuing their academic or professional careers can provide assessments of the extent to which their programs provided them the knowledge and skills they need for their careers. In addition, they can indicate the areas that need greater or lesser emphasis in the program. The graduates can be surveyed or interviewed. Since they are now independent professionals who are not subject to the direct power of the faculty, they may be especially likely to provide frank assessments.

Preparation for Professional Practice. Yet another source of information can be found in the evaluations of supervisors and employers.

Basic Facts (Cell 9). Preparation for professional practice can be assessed from institutional data when internships or practica are part of the program. These experiences often include the evaluations of the students' supervisors, which, perhaps with some alteration, can be used to assess the program's effectiveness in preparing practitioners. The expectations must be appropriate for the level of experience and the training of the students, of course (Nyquist and Wulff, 1996). In addition, if there are regular evaluations of the success of students in their training roles, these can be compared with other information. For example, the therapeutic success with clients of graduate students in clinical psychology programs can be compared with the success of experienced therapists (Stern and Lambert, 1995).

Processes (Cell 10). Students who are in the midst of their programs can be surveyed or interviewed for their views on the relevance and power of program experiences in developing professional competence. Depending on the discipline and the composition of the student group, these judgments may be better informed than they initially appear to be. That is, many professionally oriented programs attract students who already have experience as a working professional. (For example, many graduate management programs require students to have some business experience.) Another source of evaluations can be obtained from the judgments of panels of working professionals. For example, a group of experienced and successful practicing professionals could be asked to evaluate the curriculum and the content of specific courses; they could also interview current students for their judgments of the effectiveness of the program, as seen in the students' competence.

Outcomes at Completion (Cell 11). Information on the extent to which the program has successfully prepared the student for professional practice can be obtained from surveys or interviews of students completing their programs. External experts can also be employed to evaluate the students.

Long-Range Outcomes (Cell 12). The views of practicing graduates are particularly relevant in the area of professional practice. The same procedures as used in Cell 8 can be used here.

Preparation for Research and Inquiry. The following information can be collected to assess how well an advanced-degree program is preparing its students in the areas of research and inquiry.

Basic Facts (Cell 13). Assessments of program impact on student preparation for research can be obtained by procedures similar to those for Cell 9. In particular, programs that have a high percentage of students with research assistantships can use or develop assessments of the students' research skills as part of regular performance evaluations. Factors to be evaluated might be the quality of literature reviews, research designs, data collection, quantitative or qualitative analyses, interpretation of results and writing skills (Nyquist and Wulff, 1996). When appropriate to the field, records of the number and quality of publications by students could be examined. These data could be obtained from students' self-reports, with considerable accuracy (Baird and Knapp, 1981).

Processes (Cell 14). In addition to the survey and interview procedures outlined in Cells 2, 6, and 10, information about preparation for research could be obtained by gathering behavioral samples of literature reviews, research designs, and so forth. These can be evaluated for their evidence about students' effectiveness in using their time, designing studies, collecting data, creativity, and potential contribution to the field, among other things.

Outcomes (Cell 15). The same procedures used in Cells 7 and 11 can be followed.

Long-Range Outcomes (Cell 16). In addition to the procedures followed in Cells 8 and 12, the publication records of graduates can be obtained by surveys of alumni, or through abstract services such as *Psychological Abstracts* and the *Social Science Citation Index.* The latter source can be particularly useful, since it allows analyses and comparisons on several dimensions, especially the extent to which the publications of graduates are cited by other scholars in the discipline.

Preparation for Teaching. The following information can be used to assess students' preparation for teaching.

Basic Facts (Cell 17). Information on the extent to which students are prepared to teach can be obtained from a number of institutional data sets. The most obvious are student ratings of teaching assistants. Although student ratings of instruction are the subject of many myths and half-truths, by and large they are reliable, reasonably valid, relatively uncontaminated by bias, and seen as useful (Feldman, 1996). These ratings can be analyzed by comparing teaching assistants with experienced professors in the discipline and, more importantly, the degree to which teaching assistants' ratings improve as they progress through the program. The latter trend provides evidence that the program is preparing students for teaching rather than letting them flounder.

Processes (Cell 18). Information on the program's effectiveness in preparing students for teaching can be obtained from students in the midst of their programs by following many of the same procedures used in Cells 10 and 14. In addition, a variety of other sources of information can be employed, including students' self-perceptions, performance of undergraduates on common examinations, perceptions of peers, classroom observations, and portfolios. (Nyquist and Wulff, 1996, discuss these methods and their appropriate use). All of these methods need to be used as a part of a system for improving the quality of instruction, of course (Wright, and Associates, 1995).

Outcomes at Completion (Cell 19). Many of the procedures found in Cells 7, 12, and 15 can be pursued. Information on the teaching success of graduating students can also be obtained by any records of teaching awards or recognitions that they report in surveys.

Long-Range Outcomes (Cell 20). Many of the procedures followed in Cells 8, 12, and 16 can be followed. Since the purpose of assessments of progress toward outcomes is program evaluation and improvement, the open-ended suggestions of graduates who are pursuing active teaching careers are especially relevant. That is, alumni who are teaching in a variety of professional settings will have a wealth of experiences to call upon to make recommendations to their alma mater.

Comparing the Methods

The information collection methods outlined above are designed to meet different purposes and, correspondingly, have different advantages and disadvantages. This section compares the methods in terms of cost and time.

Institutional Data. These data are often the quickest and cheapest sources of information. Certainly, some institutional information forms a base of facts that are essential, such as percentage of degree completions and time-to-degree. However, as discussed in other sources (Baird, 1993), the actual cost and complexity of the effort would depend on the nature of the institution's records. In some institutions, extensive histories of students are readily available in a computerized central file. At others, the data are scattered around the institution, so the task would be to coordinate files. In the worst cases, the institution keeps the records for graduate students in individual folders, so that data for all but the most rudimentary information must be hand-coded by going through voluminous files. Once the data have been assembled, student progress can be assessed by following the procedures described by Isaac (1993). Again, to understand the processes that work, it may be important to disaggregate the data and conduct separate analyses by discipline, gender, age, and so on.

On the specific issue of doctoral time-to-degree, the easiest and quickest action is to obtain the National Research Council tapes of doctoral recipients for the institutional researcher's institution as described by Ploskonka (1993). The most recent ten-year span of data for one's institution should provide sufficient cases for subgroup analyses and the charting of trends. One can compare the time-to-degree figures for discipline, gender, source of financial support, number of dependents, age group, and other variables suggested by research and theory, as illustrated by Abedi and Benkin (1987) and by Ploskonka (1993). These comparisons can be provided very rapidly.

Surveys. Surveys of current students, graduating students, alumni, and such groups as employers are a relatively inexpensive option. They can be designed to address whatever issues are important to the program or institution. Whatever the issues that the survey addresses, it should also consider variables that studies of graduate education have shown to be important: discipline, age, sources of support, marital status, number of dependents, type of employment (off-campus related to studies, off-campus unrelated to studies, on-campus nonacademic, research assistantships, teaching assistantships), number of hours worked, fellowship status, citizenship, dates of bachelor's degree and start of graduate study, undergraduate discipline, undergraduate institution, undergraduate grades, and graduate grades. Variables suggested by models of graduate student progress include the quality of interactions with faculty and peers, confidence in one's intellectual abilities, stage of academic career, sense of mastery of the research approaches of the discipline, supportiveness of spouse, employer and other groups, commitment to the discipline, commitment to obtaining the degree, relationships with advisers, and the economic and personal significance of obtaining the degree (Baird, 1993). Information about departmental practices can be obtained from questions about the clarity and logical sequence of requirements, the extent of attempts to orient new students, whether a master's degree is required for entrance to doctoral studies, the extent to which students' progress is monitored, and the amount of departmental and university red tape. Institutional researchers whose experience in the development of questionnaires is limited can consult texts on questionnaire design and surveying. The volumes by Converse and Presser (1986), who provide counsel on simplicity, wording, alternatives, and processing, and by Dillman (1978), who provides advice on all stages of mail and telephone surveying, are particularly recommended. Of course, it would be wise to ask groups that have a stake in graduate education, including the graduate school, departmental directors of graduate study, and graduate student associations, to review a draft questionnaire and suggest improvements. The preparation and dissemination of reports can follow the suggestions of Baird (1980).

The advantages of surveys include their flexibility, breadth, and speed, as well as the access they provide to people who otherwise would be difficult to reach, such as alumni and employees. The disadvantages include the low response rate of surveys, possible bias of respondents, and the possible unwillingness of respondents to report their candid responses. However, care in the construction of the survey (including open-ended and forced-choice questions) and vigorous pursuit of the sample can lessen these disadvantages.

Interviews. Interviews are even more flexible than surveys, allowing for follow-up questions and the full exploration of the topics addressed. They can obtain information on the same topics as surveys, as just outlined. The disadvantages include the need for direct contact, which, especially with groups such as alumni, may be difficult; the considerable time and personnel costs involved; and the unwillingness of some of the interviewees to reveal their real views in a face-to-face setting. However, the disadvantages can be lessened by carefully planning the interviews, using trained interviewers and interviewing groups in addition to, or instead of, individuals.

External Evaluators. Expert, unbiased assessments of the impact of the program on students can be obtained from panels of external evaluators. Faculty in the discipline from other institutions can examine the program's curriculum, policies, and specific procedures from the perspective of other institutions' practices and their knowledge of the field. As experts in the discipline, they can also evaluate students' mastery of the field and connect what the program does to student outcomes. An important issue is the orientation of the panel; the approach should be probing but constructive, with the goal of improving the program rather than finding things to criticize. One way to ensure this orientation is the development of a consortium of scholars in the discipline. A group of faculty from similar programs could develop a round-robin series of evaluations; each institution would be visited and evaluated every several years. Such an exchange of ideas and information about specific practices could be extremely valuable. (See Wergin, 1991, for general guidelines on using external experts; the chapter by Garth and Rehulic is particularly relevant.)

Longitudinal Studies. Perhaps the most comprehensive and involved approach to assessing the influence of programs in graduate student outcomes is to begin a longitudinal study of graduate students. Institutional records could be combined with an entrance survey concerning students' backgrounds, initial plans, commitments, and views of their discipline. Retention, progress toward the degree, and movement toward learning outcomes could be studied after one year. Among master's students, degree completion and other criteria could be studied after two years. Yearly or biennial surveys of students' experiences and views would be the source of an understanding of the factors involved in student progress and growth. The details of any such study would need to be worked out, but the eventual outcomes should be specific changes in policies and practices. A sophisticated example of the kinds of analyses that could be done with such a study can be found in Nora and Cabrera (1993).

Using Assessments of Outcomes

For many years, the "outcomes" of graduate education were described with the grandiose rhetoric found in college catalogues. In more recent times, there have been attempts to make the goals more specific and, importantly, related to educational programs. Dressel (1976), although writing about undergraduate education, summarized the logic:

> If students are expected to develop a degree of independence in pursuit of learning, reach a satisfactory level of skill in communication, demonstrate sensitivity to their own values and those of their associates, become capable of collaborating with peers in defining and resolving problems, be able to recognize the relevance of their increasing knowledge to the current scene, and seek continually for insightful understanding and organization of their total educational experience, these outcomes must be specifically stated. In addition, they must be made explicit in relation to learning experiences and by providing opportunities for demonstration of the developing behavior and for evaluation of it. Content, subject matter, and behavior are interrelated and must be construed by teachers, students and evaluators. This requires an interrelated trinity of conceptual statements defining the objectives of operational statements, indicating how the behavior is to be evoked and appraised, and providing standards for deciding whether progress is evident and whether accomplishment is finally satisfactory. [p. 103]

More recent writers have emphasized the importance of making the goals specific, of linking them to specific curricular and co-curricular programs, developing methods for assessment, and evaluating students' degrees of progress toward the goals. By combining information about student characteristics, the practices and the environment of programs, and student progress toward career and learning outcomes, researchers can understand their programs much better. Of course, the key to the utility of any information is the extent to which it affects actual behavior. The kinds of studies discussed here are useful mainly in improving the quality of the decisions that are made. Such studies enable the decision maker to improve his or her understanding of what is happening in graduate education and thereby to understand the consequences of current policies or programs, plan new actions realistically, and anticipate the outcomes of future decisions accurately. At a minimum, graduate programs can be designed to meet the educational needs of academic fields more effectively and more humanely. By examining the effects of programs on students, as described by appropriate studies, the fields could at least eliminate features of their practices that are irrelevant to their pursuit of excellence or that even interfere with that pursuit, as Hartnett and Katz (1977) have suggested. Ideally, such examinations could lead to more effective, less stressful, and more stimulating programs, which would lead to an absorbing expression of students' highest potential.

LEONARD L. BAIRD *is professor of higher education at Ohio State University.*

*A number of suggestions are offered for assessment-related research
and practice in advanced-degree programs.*

Assessment in Graduate
and Professional Education:
Present Realities, Future Prospects

Jennifer Grant Haworth

For the past several years, I have watched the assessment movement blaze a trail
through our nation's colleges and universities. Sometimes I have stood in awe,
marveling at the rapid pace at which legislators and trustees have mandated
assessment across the country. At other times, my reaction has bordered on dis-
belief as I have observed faculty and administrators use assessment to turn their
"working spaces into learning places" focused on the improvement of student
learning (Angelo, 1996). At still other times, assessment's political overtures have
put me squarely on guard. Over the last few years, however, I must admit that
my most common response to the assessment movement has been one of befud-
dled astonishment. On all too many occasions, I have wondered how a movement so fundamentally involved in research and discovery could spread like
wildfire throughout undergraduate education but barely cause a flicker in graduate and professional education. It appears that the recent assessment movement has ignored not only the most expensive component of our nation's higher
education system, but also the most influential in terms of its contributions to
the advancement of knowledge and the development of future leaders.

In this concluding chapter, I draw on writings from this volume and elsewhere to give institutional researchers an understanding of the present realities
of and future potential for assessment in graduate and professional education.
Toward this end, I begin with my observations on the current state of assessment in our nation's advanced-degree programs. I then offer an agenda for assessment-related research and practice in graduate and professional education.

Observations on the "Assessment Movement" in Graduate and Professional Education

In a recent article in the *AAHE Bulletin,* Thomas Angelo, director of the AAHE's Assessment Forum, opined that at least when viewed from a "purely quantitative perspective," the assessment movement has been, "a smashing success" (1996, p. 3). He supported his judgment with several pieces of evidence, including, for example, that "more than 90 percent of all U.S. campuses" have planned for or engaged in some form of systematic assessment activity and that all six regional accrediting associations—as well as several field-specific accrediting bodies—now include assessment-related requirements in their guidelines.

As I mentioned earlier, however, the assessment movement to which Angelo and so many others refer has been largely an undergraduate phenomenon. Except for several states that require publicly funded universities to conduct regular program reviews of their graduate and professional programs, a systematic approach to ongoing assessment—particularly of student learning outcomes—has been virtually nonexistent at the postbaccalaureate level. From my reading of the literature, I discovered few programs and institutions involved in graduate and professional education that took the charge of the undergraduate assessment movement seriously: to develop an "ongoing process aimed at understanding and improving student learning. . . . [that] involves making our expectations explicit and public; setting appropriate criteria and high standards for learning quality; systematically gathering, analyzing, and interpreting evidence to determine how well performance matches those expectations and standards; and using the resulting information to document, explain, and improve performance" (Angelo, 1996, p. 3).

This neglect of assessment-related activity and research in postbaccalaureate programs is, indeed, unfortunate. For as several scholars have noted, there is a "crying need" (Baird, 1988, p. 109) for such information. In the map he sketched of postsecondary assessment nearly a decade ago, for example, Leonard L. Baird (1988) pointed out just how little we know about graduate and professional education in this country. As he explained, although the literature contains a "handful of studies of the factors influencing attendance in graduate and professional school, attrition in graduate school, and the graduate and professional school experience," far more research is needed in these and other areas (1988, p. 109). Nearly ten years later, several authors in this volume have reaffirmed Baird's conclusion. For instance, while Linda Serra Hagedorn and Amaury Nora located several studies related to the predictive validity of the Graduate Record Examination (GRE), they found little to no empirical research on how other admissions-related variables, such as student motivation or work-related professional experience, might more accurately predict student success (measured in any number of ways) in advanced-degree programs. In much the same vein, in their chapter on doctoral student retention, Maresi Nerad and Debra Sands Miller note that despite a growing interest in this area, we know far too little about those factors that contribute to student attrition and retention in postbaccalaureate programs. And in exploring the literature on the "outcomes" of graduate and professional education, Anne E. Bilder and Clifton F. Conrad found, regrettably, that the literature offers few insights into the impact that graduate and professional study has on students.

Considering the paucity of assessment-related research, writing, and practice, it is no small wonder that former Harvard University president Derek Bok once called graduate education the "soft underbelly" of American universities (Bowen and Rudenstine, 1992). The writings in this volume—particularly when coupled with others (Baird, 1988; Baird, 1990; Haworth, 1996; Malaney, 1988)—underscore the need for more assessment-related activity in graduate and professional education. To be sure, institutional researchers can play a vital role in meeting this need, as I will discuss shortly.

Agenda for Assessment-Related Research and Practice in Graduate and Professional Education

Karl Schilling and Karen Maitland Schilling have stated that in order "to change or improve an invisible system, one must first make it visible" (1993, p. 172). Such a task, of course, involves far more than throwing pixie dust on a program or waving a magic wand over a data set. Rather, it requires us to peer inside our own and others' programs in order to understand what goes on inside of them, how, and with what effects. Taking this idea to heart and drawing on insights gleaned from the preceding chapters as well as in other literatures, I have identified several currently underdeveloped but potentially fruitful arenas for future inquiry and practice in graduate and professional education. For each, I briefly describe the arena for assessment, note its limitations, and discuss possible implications for institutional research and practice.

Arena One: Demand for Graduate and Professional Education. Currently, institutional researchers rely upon a handful of national databases to monitor national shifts in demand for graduate and professional education. Four general types of databases are available: (1) those that monitor changes in the demographic profile of graduate and professional students (such as the National Center for Education Statistics [NCES] IPEDS Fall Enrollment Survey); (2) those that track shifts in student demand for advanced degrees across various fields of study (including data found in the NCES *Digest of Educational Statistics* [1995]); (3) those that provide information on undergraduate students' interests in and applications to graduate and professional programs (such as the UCLA Higher Education Research Institute's annual survey on freshman attitudes, which includes data on students' attitudes toward attending graduate or professional school, and the NCES Baccalaureate and Beyond Longitudinal database that collects data on graduate and professional school applications); and, finally, (4) those that project labor force demands for professional occupations (the Bureau of Labor Statistics publishes such forecasts on a regular basis).

In Chapter Two, Peter D. Syverson refers to several of these sources, as he documents national shifts in student and labor force demand for graduate and professional education. These databases are useful for this purpose, providing a broad perspective on who is most likely to seek advanced degrees in what fields of study in the not-so-distant future. Yet, since most of us operate within certain regional and local market sectors, these data give us only one part of the story. We sorely need research that systematically examines shifts in student and labor force demand for master's, doctoral, and first-professional degrees across fields of study by geographic region and, ideally, by locality. This objective can be accomplished in any number of ways: through single-institution case studies, inter-institutional regional consortia that collect local student and labor force demand data and disseminate it via regional databases, and the inclusion of disaggregated regional data in many of the aforementioned national databases.

Besides our lack of systematic information on broader shifts in demand by region and locale, another ripe area for future investigation pertains to how institutions respond to shifts in their local and regional markets. Besides collecting data on enrollment, for example, research is needed that explores the extent to which institutions adjust their undergraduate and graduate curricular offerings, delivery systems (particularly those using "nontraditional" formats), and pedagogical practices to accommodate shifts in clientele. Have these adjustments occurred? Which have met with success? Failure? Surely, if more students are, as Syverson tells us, working professionals who pursue graduate study on a part-time basis, then information on institutional responses to this particular clientele could be quite beneficial to many in the graduate and professional education community. Institutional researchers can fill this void through many different approaches: conducting document reviews to assess curricular changes; interviewing administrators and faculty to determine the changes they have made to meet new market and clientele demands; and constructing employer, alumni, and student surveys to evaluate the extent and effectiveness of various marketing strategies and programmatic responses. Regardless of the approach taken, there is a compelling need for multi- and single-institution studies in this arena.

Arena Two: Graduate and Professional School Admissions Criteria. As Linda Serra Hagedorn and Amaury Nora show in Chapter Three, there is an increasing body of evidence documenting that conventional admissions criteria—including undergraduate grade point averages and standardized exams—are only marginally predictive of student success in advanced-degree programs. Such criteria, they note, rely exclusively on a unidimensional conceptualization of student success as academic achievement. Other indicators of success, such as student retention to graduation or the development of professional competencies and attitudes, are completely ignored. To be sure, prognostication is always risky, but it is so much more risky when based exclusively on a single criterion. Given the multiple skills, talents, and experiences that are often necessary for success in advanced-degree programs, there is a strong need to rethink and expand the admissions criteria that faculty use in these programs.

Institutional researchers can play at least two important roles here. First, they can work in concert with faculty and administrators to identify factors that they believe are illustrative of successful student performance at the master's, doctoral, or first-professional degree levels. As Hagedorn and Nora suggest in their conceptual framework, these may include factors related to academic achievement, professional knowledge, skills, attitudes, and behaviors, and student retention. After these have been identified, institutional researchers can assist faculty in developing admissions criteria and indicators that measure these factors. They can also offer suggestions on various methods (including admissions interviews, student oral and written critiques of research, student analyses of case studies, and so forth) to collect evidence in relation to each criterion.

Second, once developed, institutional researchers can play another equally important role by testing how well newly formulated admissions criteria predict student success. In particular, research should focus on two questions: What criteria are the "best" predictors of student success within and across fields of study and degree levels? and, Do certain criteria more accurately predict success for some students (such as minority or non-traditional students) over others? Particularly since the literature is largely silent on the predictive validity of alternative admissions criteria, we particularly need research in this area.

To be sure, institutional researchers can undertake several other important future tasks in this area (including the need to develop highly efficient, cost-effective application forms, questionnaires, and coding-scoring rubrics for assessing students during the admissions process). That said, the two mentioned above deserve special attention on intellectual, financial, and ethical grounds.

Arena Three: Quality in Advanced-Degree Programs. In contrast to the previously discussed assessment arenas, a considerable amount of research has been conducted on program quality in advanced-degree programs, with the bulk of it examining quality in doctoral education. As Baird, Haworth, and Conrad note in earlier chapters, however, most of this research has focused on measuring reputation rather than quality, per se. While useful as far as they go, these studies ignore the primacy of student learning in their assessments of quality. In Chapter Four, Haworth and Conrad describe their recently developed "engagement theory of program quality"—a theory that, in their words, "refocuses quality assessment on student learning." Largely because their work provides an alternative to several prevailing views of quality in the literature, it raises several possibilities for future research on program quality in graduate and professional education.

Perhaps the most obvious of these is that the theory—the first such theory of quality in the higher education literature—posits many new theoretical linkages that require additional testing and validation. Such a task demands the development of appropriate indicators that would allow institutional researchers and others to test the validity of the theory's stated relationships among attributes, learning experiences, and student outcomes. While quantitative analyses would be particularly useful for larger, multi-institutional and cross-disciplinary investigations, qualitative case studies of smaller scope should also occupy an important place on the agenda. Regardless of the type of study undertaken, it is imperative that any future testing of the theory include the perspectives of multiple stakeholders.

The applicability and validity of the theory across degree levels provides institutional researchers and scholars with another ripe area for future investigation. Although developed on the basis of interviews held with nearly eight hundred faculty, administrators, students, alumni, and employers involved in master's-level education, Haworth and Conrad contend that their theory may also hold explanatory power at the undergraduate and doctoral levels. To be sure, the engagement theory finds considerable support in several literatures (Haworth and Conrad, 1997, pp. 206–212). Nonetheless, the theory should be subjected to further testing at the undergraduate, first-professional, and doctoral degree levels.

Additionally, there is a strong need to develop efficient and cost-effective assessment tools based on the theory. Interview protocols and survey instruments specifically tailored for different audiences (current students, alumni, faculty, administrators, and employers) are especially needed. These and other instruments will require the creation of reliable indicators for each of the theory's attributes that, ideally, should include both quantitative and qualitative measures.

Arena Four: Student Persistence. An increasing amount of research on student persistence in graduate and professional education has recently found its way into the literature. The vast majority of these studies have examined doctoral student attrition, largely ignoring the issue at the master's and first-professional levels. This is not surprising for, as Maresi Nerad and Debra Sands Miller point out in Chapter Five, an increasing number of state policy makers have begun to pressure graduate schools for more detailed reports on doctoral time-to-degree and student completion rates. And while recent research in this arena has been illuminating (particularly in doctoral education), there is still much more that we need to learn.

Besides giving institutional researchers many keen insights into the factors that influence doctoral student persistence, Nerad and Miller's research at the University of California-Berkeley also suggests several promising new areas for future research. Perhaps the most obvious of these is the need to examine more systematically the linkages between graduate student retention and institutional and departmental cultures, policies, and practices. As Nerad and Miller's research indicates, doctoral student attrition is seldom the result of academic failure; rather, a combination of several other factors—including student frustration with academic policies and procedures, student disappointment with program offerings and faculty advising, and student experiences with an inhospitable departmental climate—are much more likely to contribute to the decision to leave graduate study. There is an urgent need for research that both subjects these factors and their relationship to student attrition to more testing and seeks to identify other factors (individual, institutional, departmental, or external) that affect student completion rates.

There is also a need to investigate how various factors, including many that scholars have previously identified (see, for example, Nerad and Cerny,

1993), may differentially affect the persistence of subgroups of students in diverse settings. For instance, do men and women attribute their decision to leave or complete graduate or professional school to similar factors? Are different factors at play that affect the retention of older, returning adult students as opposed to traditional-aged students? Part-time versus full-time students? Students in professional fields of study versus those in the traditional arts and sciences? Additionally, other questions merit attention, including the need to examine whether factors related to student persistence may vary by field of study, degree level (master's, doctoral, first-professional), and program delivery (day, evening, weekend, satellite). Qualitative approaches to inquiry that draw upon the perspectives of various students in diverse contexts are especially well-suited to these kinds of initial, comparative analyses, for they allow researchers to understand more fully the meanings that both "completers" and "leavers" attach to various aspects of their graduate and professional school experiences. Not surprisingly, these studies are likely to have greater utility if they incorporate longitudinal designs (Tinto, 1993).

Nerad and Miller's chapter has other implications for institutional researchers as well. Foremost among them is the need to develop institutional databases that track the progress of advanced-degree students—whether at the master's, doctoral, or first-professional level. Databases of this sort can provide faculty and administrators with an empirical basis for understanding "normal degree progress" for diverse subgroups of students in different fields of study and types of degree programs (Baird, 1988). Moreover, since monitoring student completion rates in advanced-degree programs is a relatively new development, there is also a need to construct student persistence surveys and other instruments of related interest that can assist faculty and administrators in assessing this important outcome.

Arena Five: Student Outcomes of Graduate and Professional Education. Nerad and Miller write:

> While universities can usefully monitor time-to-degree and completion rates and be aware of any trends, focusing on such quantifiable measures alone neglects an essential and unquantifiable outcome of graduate education: the formation of a cultured mind. This valuable outcome can occur regardless of whether the doctoral program has been completed or employment found in the specific field in which the degree was completed.

Their comment underscores the importance of documenting the outcomes of graduate and professional study, whether related to knowledge and skills development, degree completion, job placement, or long-term professional success. Yet, as Baird, Bilder, and Conrad all note, although a strong warrant for studies of this sort exist, few scholars have conducted research in this area. The lack of research on student learning outcomes in master's and doctoral programs is especially troubling.

We urgently need empirical studies that systematically explore those outcomes—learning and otherwise—associated with advanced-degree study in

U.S. colleges and universities. Specifically, the following questions could yield valuable information to several stakeholder audiences:

What have graduates learned because of their enrollment in this advanced-degree program?
How have graduates changed because of their enrollment in this advanced-degree program?
How do different student subgroups in this department—in terms of age, sex, race-ethnicity, part- and full-time status, and years of professional, nonuniversity workplace experience—compare in terms of various outcomes, including knowledge and skills outcomes, completion rates, and job placement?
What are the career paths of recent program graduates, and how do these differ by degree level and disciplinary specialization?

Ideally, such research should not only identify student outcomes but also the processes, or experiences, that contributed to them. Moreover, as Baird reminds us, studies of this sort should also consider institutional and student pre-entry characteristics. While longitudinal designs are most likely to yield the useful information, other designs—including cross-sectional investigations and case studies—can provide important starting points for future research.

There are several tasks that institutional researchers could perform in this assessment arena. For starters, they could work with faculty within specific departments to clarify those outcomes that they most expect students to "learn and be able to do" in their programs and then design various assessment protocols designed to measure these outcomes. Certainly, Baird's assessment framework could be used as a starting point for thinking about categories of learning outcomes; his description of various methods and accompanying measures could also make actual assessment efforts less cumbersome. Institutional researchers could also develop various assessment instruments that faculty could use to collect information on student outcomes within their respective disciplines, including exit interview protocols and student, alumni, and employer surveys. Finally, institutional researchers have an important role to play when it comes to compiling and coordinating data, particularly in terms of developing and maintaining institutional databases and records. As faculty and others conduct student outcomes assessment studies, every effort should be made to record results into an institutional database. The compilation of such data can then lead to comparative evaluation studies over time (both within and across departments), thereby producing useful aggregate institutional data on student outcomes.

Conclusion

Several years ago, Patrick Terenzini quipped that "assessment requires that we try to understand whether the things we do and believe to be educational in fact produce the intended outcomes" (in Stark and Thomas, 1994, p. 524). At this time, it appears that past practice and belief rule the day in graduate and professional programs. To be sure, knowledge of this type has its place, but it does not—and should not—serve as a substitute for ongoing, systematic inquiry. Ongoing assessment, while not a panacea, can provide faculty, administrators, and institutional researchers with useful data on what goes on inside of programs, how teaching and learning occur, and with what effects. Armed with this information, decision makers can then go about the task of developing policies and practices that will, ultimately, improve student learning.

JENNIFER GRANT HAWORTH is assistant professor of higher education at Loyola University Chicago.

REFERENCES

Abbott, W. F. "University and Departmental Determinants of the Prestige of Sociology Departments." *American Sociologist,* 1972, *7,* 14–15.

Abbott, W. F., and Barlow, H. M. "Stratification Theory and Organizational Rank: Resources, Functions, and University Prestige in the United States." *Pacific Sociological Review,* 1972, *15,* 401–424.

Abedi, J., and Benkin, E. "The Effects of Students' Academic, Financial, and Demographic Variables on Time to Doctorate." *Research in Higher Education,* 1987, *17,* 3–14.

American Bar Association, Section of Legal Education and Admissions to the Bar. *A Review of Legal Education in the United States: Fall 1995.* Indianapolis, Ind.: American Bar Association, 1995.

American College Personnel Association (ACPA). *The Student Learning Imperative: Implications for Student Affairs.* Alexandria, Va.: ACPA, 1994.

Anderson, M. *Impostors in the Temple: American Intellectuals Are Destroying Our Universities and Cheating Our Students of Their Future.* New York: Simon & Schuster, 1992.

Anderson, M. S., Louis, K. S., and Earle, J. "Disciplinary and Departmental Effects on Observations of Faculty and Graduate Student Misconduct." *Journal of Higher Education,* 1994, *65,* 331–350.

Angelo, T. A. "Transforming Assessment: High Standards for Higher Learning." *AAHE Bulletin,* 1996, *48* (8), 3–4.

Arrow, K. J. "Excellence and Equity in Higher Education." *Education Economics,* 1993, *1* (1), 5–12.

Association of Governing Boards of Universities and Colleges (AGB). *Trustees and Troubled Times in Higher Education.* Washington, D.C.: AGB, 1992.

Astin, A. W. *Four Critical Years: Effects of College on Beliefs, Attitudes, and Knowledge.* San Francisco: Jossey-Bass, 1977.

Astin, A. W. *Achieving Educational Excellence.* San Francisco: Jossey-Bass, 1985.

Astin, A. W. *What Matters in College: Four Critical Years Revisited.* San Francisco: Jossey-Bass, 1993.

Baird, L. L. "Using Campus Surveys for Improving Colleges." In L. L. Baird, R. T. Hartnett, and Associates (eds.), *Understanding Student and Faculty Life.* San Francisco: Jossey-Bass, 1980.

Baird, L. L. "A Map of Postsecondary Assessment." *Research in Higher Education,* 1988, *28* (2), 99–115.

Baird, L. L. "The Melancholy of Anatomy: The Personal and Professional Development of Graduate and Professional School Students." In J. C. Smart (ed.), *Higher Education: Handbook of Theory and Research,* Vol. 6. New York: Agathon Press, 1990.

Baird, L. L. "Publication Productivity in Doctoral Research Departments: Interdisciplinary and Intradisciplinary Factors." *Research in Higher Education,* 1991, *32,* 303–318.

Baird, L. L. (ed.). *Increasing Graduate Student Retention and Degree Attainment.* New Directions for Institutional Research, no. 80. San Francisco: Jossey-Bass, 1993.

Baird, L. L., and Knapp, J. C. *The Inventory of Documented Accomplishments for Graduate Admission.* Princeton, N.J.: Graduate Record Examination Board, 1981.

Banta, T. W., and Associates. *Making a Difference: Outcomes of a Decade of Assessment in Higher Education.* San Francisco: Jossey-Bass, 1993.

Barr, R. B., and Tagg, J. "From Teaching to Learning: A New Paradigm for Undergraduate Education." *Change,* 1995, *27,* 12–25.

Benkin, E. *Where Have All the Doctoral Students Gone? A Study of Doctoral Student Attrition at UCLA.* Unpublished doctoral dissertation, Department of Education, University of California, Los Angeles, 1984.

Berelson, B. *Graduate Education in the United States.* New York: McGraw-Hill, 1960.

Bergquist, W. *Quality Through Access, Access With Quality: The New Imperative for Higher Education.* San Francisco: Jossey-Bass, 1995.

Beyer, J. M., and Snipper, R. "Objective Versus Subjective Indicators of Quality." *Sociology of Education,* 1974, 47, 541–557.

Biglan, A. "The Characteristics of Subject Matter in Different Academic Areas." *Journal of Applied Psychology,* 1973a, 57 (3), 195–203.

Biglan, A. "Relationships Between Subject Matter Characteristics and the Structure and Output of University Departments." *Journal of Applied Psychology,* 1973b, 57 (3), 204–213.

Blackburn, R. T., and Lingenfelter, P. E. *Assessing Quality for Doctoral Programs: Criteria and Correlates of Excellence.* Ann Arbor: Center for the Study of Higher Education, University of Michigan, 1973.

Bok, D. *Beyond the Ivory Tower: Social Responsibilities of the Modern University.* Cambridge, Mass.: Harvard University Press, 1982.

Bok, D. *Higher Learning.* Cambridge, Mass.: Harvard University Press, 1986.

Borchert, M.A.E. *Master's Education: A Guide for Faculty and Administrators: A Policy Statement.* Washington, D.C.: Council of Graduate Schools, 1994.

Borden, V.M.H., and Banta, T. W. (eds.). *Using Performance Indicators to Guide Strategic Decision Making.* New Directions for Institutional Research, no. 82. San Francisco: Jossey-Bass, 1994.

Botrill, K. V., and Borden, V.M.H. "Appendix: Examples from the Literature." In V.M.H. Borden and T. W. Banta (eds.), *Using Performance Indicators to Guide Strategic Decision Making.* New Directions for Institutional Research, no. 82. San Francisco: Jossey-Bass, 1994.

Bowen, W. G., and Rudenstine, N. L. *In Pursuit of the Ph.D.* Princeton, N.J.: Princeton University Press, 1992.

Brazziel, M. E. *Correlates of Program Entry and Completion Time of Humanities Doctorate Recipients.* Report completed under Contract P-20236. Washington, D.C.: National Endowment for the Humanities, 1984.

Brazziel, W. F. "Older Students and Doctoral Production." *Review of Higher Education,* 1992, 15 (4), 449–462.

Brown, S. V., Clewell, B. C., Ekstrom, R. B., Goertz, M. E., and Powers, D. E. *Research Agenda for the Graduate Record Examinations Board Minority Graduate Education Project: An Update.* Princeton, N.J.: Educational Testing Service, 1994.

Bureau of Labor Statistics, U.S. Department of Labor. *Employment Outlook: 1994–2005 Job Quality and Other Aspects of Projected Employment Growth.* Bulletin 2472. Washington, D.C.: Government Printing Office, 1995.

Bureau of Labor Statistics, U.S. Department of Labor. *Occupational Outlook Handbook: 1996–97 Edition.* Bulletin 2470. Washington, D.C.: Government Printing Office, 1996.

Carter, D. J., and Wilson, R. *Eighth Annual Status Report on Minorities in Higher Education.* Washington, D.C.: American Council on Education, 1992.

Cartter, A. M. *An Assessment of Quality in Graduate Education.* Washington, D.C.: American Council on Education, 1966.

Chickering, A. W., and Gamson, Z. F. "Seven Principles for Good Practice in Undergraduate Education." *AAHE Bulletin,* 1987, 39, 3–7.

Chronicle of Higher Education. "Earned Degrees Conferred by U. S. Institutions, 1992–93." *Chronicle of Higher Education,* June 9, 1995, p. A37.

Clark, M. J. "The Meaning of Quality in Graduate and Professional Education." In J. Katz and R. T. Hartnett (eds.), *Scholars in the Making: The Development of Professional Students.* Cambridge, Mass.: Ballinger, 1976.

Clark, M. J. *Older and Younger Graduate Students: A Comparison of Goals, Grades, and GRE scores.* GRE Board Research Report GREB 81–17R/ETS Research Report 84–5. Princeton, N.J.: Educational Testing Service, 1984.

Clark, M. J., Hartnett, R. T., and Baird, L. L. *Assessing Dimensions of Quality in Doctoral Education: A Technical Report of a National Study in Three Fields.* Princeton, N.J.: Educational Testing Service, 1976.

Clemente, F., and Sturgis, R. B. "Quality of Departments of Doctoral Training and Research Productivity." *Sociology of Education,* 1974, *47,* 287–299.

Collins, R. *The Credential Society: An Historical Sociology of Education and Stratification.* Orlando, Fla.: Academic Press, 1979.

Conrad, C. F., and Blackburn, R. T. "Correlates of Departmental Quality in Regional Colleges and Universities." *American Educational Research Journal,* 1985a, *22,* 279–295.

Conrad, C. F., and Blackburn, R. T. "Research on Program Quality: A Review and Critique of the Literature." In J. C. Smart (ed.), *Higher Education: Handbook of Theory and Research,* Vol. 1. New York: Agathon Press, 1985b.

Conrad, C. F., and Blackburn, R. T. "Current Views of Departmental Quality: An Empirical Examination." *Review of Higher Education,* 1986, *9,* 249–265.

Conrad, C. F., Haworth, J. G., and Millar, S. B. *A Silent Success: Master's Education in the United States.* Baltimore, Md.: Johns Hopkins University Press, 1993.

Conrad, C. F., and Pratt, A. M. "Designing for Quality." *Journal of Higher Education,* 1985, *56,* 601–622.

Conrad, C. F., and Wilson, R. F. *Academic Program Reviews.* ASHE-ERIC Higher Education Research Report, no. 5. Washington, D.C.: American Association for Higher Education, 1985.

Converse, J. M., and Presser, S. *Survey Questions: Handcrafting the Standardized Questionnaire.* Thousand Oaks, Calif.: Sage, 1986.

Cook, M., and Swanson, A. "The Interaction of Student and Program Variables for the Purpose of Developing a Model for Predicting Graduation from Graduate Programs over a 10-year Period." *Research in Higher Education,* 1978, *8* (1), 83–91.

Council of Graduate Schools in the United States. *The Master's Degree: A Policy Statement.* Washington, D.C.: Council of Graduate Schools, 1981.

Council of Graduate Schools. *An Essential Guide to Graduate Admissions.* Washington, D.C.: Council of Graduate Schools, 1992.

Crane, D. "Scientists at Major and Minor Universities: A Study of Productivity and Recognition." *American Sociological Review,* Oct. 1970, *30,* 699–714.

Davis, B. G. "Demystifying Assessment: Learning from the Field of Evaluation." In P. J. Gray (ed.), *Achieving Assessment Goals Using Evaluation Techniques.* New Directions for Higher Education, no. 67. San Francisco: Jossey-Bass, 1989.

Davis, T. M. (ed.). *Open Doors 1994/95 Report on International Educational Exchange.* New York: Institute of International Education, 1995.

Day, J. C. *Population Projections of the United States by Age, Sex, Race, and Hispanic Origin: 1995 to 2050.* U.S. Bureau of the Census, Current Population Reports, P25–1130. Washington, D.C.: Government Printing Office, 1996.

Dillman, D. A. *Mail and Telephone Surveys: The Total Design Method.* New York: Wiley, 1978.

Dodge, E., and Mulvey, P. J. "1995 Initial Employment Follow-Up of 1994 Physics Degree Recipients." *AIP Report,* May 1996.

Douglas, G. H. *Education Without Impact: How Our Universities Fail the Young.* New York: Birch Lane Press, 1992.

Dressel, P. L. *Handbook of Academic Evaluation.* San Francisco: Jossey-Bass, 1976.

Drew, D. E., and Karpf, R. "Ranking Academic Departments: Empirical Findings and a Theoretical Perspective." *Research in Higher Education,* 1981, *14,* 305–320.

Elam, C. L., and Johnson, M.M.S. "Prediction of Medical Students' Academic Performance: Does the Admission Interview Help?" *Academic Medicine,* 1992, *67,* S28-S30.

Enright, M. K., and Gitomer, D. *Toward a Description of Successful Graduate Students.* GRE Board Research Report 85–17R/ETS Research Report 89–9. Princeton, N.J.: Educational Testing Service, 1989.

Ethington, C. A., and Smart, J. C. "Persistence to Graduate Education." *Research in Higher Education,* 1986, *24,* 287–303.

Ewell, P. T. "To Capture the Ineffable: New Forms of Assessment in Higher Education." In J. S. Stark and A. Thomas (eds.), *Assessment and Program Evaluation.* Needham Heights, Mass.: Simon & Schuster Custom Publishing, 1994.

Fairweather, J. S. "Reputational Quality of Academic Programs: The Institutional Halo." *Research in Higher Education,* 1988, *28,* 345–356.

Fairweather, J. S., and Brown, D. F. "Dimensions of Academic Program Quality." *Review of Higher Education,* 1991, *14,* 155–176.

Feldman, K. A. "Identifying Exemplary Teachers and Teaching: Evidence from Student Ratings." In R. P. Perry and J. C. Smart (eds.), *Effective Teaching in Higher Education: Research and Practice.* New York: Agathon Press, 1996.

Gaddy, C. D. "Overview of Current Labor Market Conditions: Employment for New Science and Engineering Ph.D.s." In A. H. Teich, S. D. Nelson, and C. McEnaney (eds.), *AAAS Science and Technology Policy Yearbook 1995.* Washington, D.C.: American Association for the Advancement of Science, 1995.

Gaither, G. H. (ed.). *Assessing Performance in an Age of Accountability: Case Studies.* New Directions for Higher Education, no. 91. San Francisco: Jossey-Bass, 1995.

Gillingham, L., Seneca, J. J., and Taussig, M. K. "The Determinants of Progress to the Doctoral Degree." *Research in Higher Education,* 1991, *32* (4), 449–468.

Girves, J. E., and Wemmerus, V. "Developing Models of Graduate School Degree Progress." *Journal of Higher Education,* 1988, *59* (2), 163–189.

Glaser, B. G., and Strauss, A. L. *The Discovery of Grounded Theory.* Chicago: Aldine, 1967.

Glazer, J. S. *The Master's Degree: Tradition, Diversity, Innovation.* ASHE-ERIC Higher Education Research Report, no. 6. Washington, D.C.: Association for the Study of Higher Education, 1986.

Golde, C. "Student Descriptions of the Doctoral Attrition Process." Paper presented at the Annual Meeting of the Association for the Study of Higher Education, Tucson, Arizona, Nov. 10–13, 1994. (ED 375 733)

Golde, C. "How Departmental Contextual Factors Shape Doctoral Student Attrition." Doctoral dissertation proposal, Stanford University, School of Education, 1995.

"Graduate and Professional Degrees Conferred by U.S. Institutions, 1992–93." *Chronicle of Higher Education,* June 9, 1995, p. A37.

Graduate Record Examinations Board. *GRE 1995–96 Guide to the Use of the Graduate Record Examinations Programs.* Princeton, N.J.: Educational Testing Service, 1995.

Gross, E. *University Goals and Academic Power.* Washington, D.C.: Office of Education, 1968.

Guskin, A. "Reducing Student Costs and Enhancing Student Learning: The University Challenge of the 1990s." *Change,* 1994, *25,* 23–29.

Hagstrom, W. O. "Inputs, Outputs, and the Prestige of University Science Departments." *Sociology of Education,* 1971, *44,* 375–397.

Hall, R. M., and Sandler, B. R. "Academic Mentoring for Women Students and Faculty: A New Look at an Old Way to Get Ahead." Washington, D.C.: Project on the Status and Education of Women, Association of American Colleges, 1983.

Hansen, W. L. "Educating and Training New Economics Ph.D.'s: How Good a Job Are We Doing?" *American Economics Review,* 1990, *80* (2), 437–450.

Hartle, T., Baratz, J., and Clark, M. J. *Older Students and the GRE Aptitude Test.* GRE Board Research Report GREB 76–13R. Princeton, N.J.: Educational Testing Service, 1983.

Hartnett, R. T., and Katz, J. "The Education of Graduate Students." *Journal of Higher Education,* 1977, *48,* 646–64.

Hathaway, J. C. "The Mythical Meritocracy of Law School Admissions." *Journal of Legal Education,* 1984, *34,* 86–96.

Haworth, J. G. "Doctoral Programs in American Higher Education." In J. C. Smart (ed.), *Higher Education: Handbook of Theory and Research,* Vol. 11. New York: Agathon Press, 1996.

Haworth, J. G., and Conrad, C. F. *Emblems of Quality in Higher Education: Developing and Sustaining High-Quality Academic Programs.* Needham Heights, Mass.: Allyn & Bacon, 1997.

Hofstadter, R., and Metzger, W. P. *The Development of Academic Freedom in the United States.* New York: Columbia University Press, 1955.

Hook, S. *Academic Freedom and Academic Anarchy.* New York: Cowles, 1969.

House, J. D. "Age Bias in Prediction of Graduate Grade Point Average from Graduate Record Examination Scores." *Educational and Psychological Measurement,* 1989, *49,* 663–666.

Huppert, F. A., and Kopelman, M. D. "Rates of Forgetting in Normal Aging: A Comparison with Dementia." *Neuropsychologia,* 1989, 27 (6), 849–860.

Isaac, P. D. "Measuring Graduate Student Retention." In L. L. Baird (ed.), *Increasing Graduate Student Retention and Degree Attainment.* New Directions for Institutional Research, no. 80. San Francisco: Jossey-Bass, 1993.

Jacks, P., Chubin, D. E., Porter, A. L., and Connolly, T. "The ABCs of ABDs: A Study of Incomplete Doctorates." *Improving College and University Teaching,* 1983, *31* (2), 74–81.

Jolly, P., and Hudley, D. M. (eds.). *AAMC Data Book: Statistical Information Related to Medical Education.* Washington, D.C.: Association of American Medical Colleges, 1995.

Jones, L. V., Lindzey, G., and Coggeshall, P. E. (eds.). *An Assessment of Research-Doctorate Programs in the United States.* (5 vols.) Washington, D.C.: National Academy Press, 1982.

Kaczmarek, M., and Franco, J. N. "Sex Differences in Prediction of Academic Performance by the Graduate Record Examination." *Psychological Reports,* 1986, *59,* 1197–1198.

Kells, H. R. *Self-Study Processes: A Guide to Self-Evaluation in Higher Education.* Phoenix, Ariz.: Oryx/American Council on Education, 1995.

Kerr, C. *The Uses of the University.* Cambridge, Mass.: Harvard University Press, 1995.

Keyishian v Board of Regents, 365 U.S. 589 (1967).

Kidder, R. M. "Graduate Education: Can It Survive?" *Christian Science Monitor,* Dec. 19, 1983, p. 21.

King, S., and Wolfe, L. "A Latent-Variable Causal Model of Faculty Reputational Ratings." *Research in Higher Education,* 1987, *27,* 99–106.

Kirkland, M. C. "The Effects of Tests on Students and Schools." *Review of Educational Research,* 1971, *41* (4), 318.

Knox, A. B. *Adult Development and Learning: A Handbook on Individual Growth and Competence in the Adult Years for Education and the Helping Professions.* San Francisco: Jossey-Bass, 1977.

Kolman, E. M., Gallagher, K. S., Hossler, D., and Catania, F. "The Outcomes of Doctoral Education: An Institutional Study." *Research in Higher Education,* 1987, *27* (2), 107–118.

Kuh, G. D *Indices of Quality in the Undergraduate Experience.* AAHE-ERIC Higher Education Research Report, no. 4. Washington, D.C.: American Association for Higher Education, 1981.

Kuh, G. D. "What Do We Do Now? Implications for Educators of 'How College Affects Students.'" *Review of Higher Education,* 1992, *15,* 349–363.

Kuh, G. D., Schuh, J. H., and Whitt, E. J. *Involving Colleges: Successful Approaches to Fostering Student Learning and Development Outside the Classroom.* San Francisco: Jossey-Bass, 1991.

Kulik, J. A., Bangert-Downs, R. L., and Kulik, C.L.C. "Effectiveness of Coaching for Aptitude Tests." *Psychological Bulletin,* 1984, *95* (2), 179–188.

Lavendar, A. D., Mathers, R. A., and Pease, J. "The Student Faculty Ratio in Graduate Programs of Selected Departments of Sociology: A Supplement to the Janes Report." *American Sociologist,* 1971, *6,* 29–30.

Lawrence, J. K., and Green, K. C. *A Question of Quality: The Higher Education Ratings Game.* AAHE-ERIC Higher Education Research Report, no. 5. Washington, D.C.: American Association for Higher Education, 1980.

Lindquist, V. R. *A Midyear Review of the Northwestern Endicott Report.* Evanston, Ill.: Northwestern University Placement Center, 1983.

Lipschutz, S. S. "Enhancing Success in Doctoral Education: From Policy to Practice." In L. L. Baird (ed.), *Increasing Graduate Student Retention and Degree Attainment.* New Directions for Institutional Research, no. 80. San Francisco: Jossey-Bass, 1993.

Lomperis, A. M. "The Demographic Transformation of American Doctoral Education." In R. G. Ehrenberg (ed.), *Research in Labor Economics,* Vol. 13. Greenwich, Conn.: JAI Press, 1992.

Long, J. B. *Factors Related to Attrition and Success in Degree and Non-Degree Doctoral Students in Education.* Ed.D. Dissertation, Northern Arizona University, 1987.

Lovitts, B. "Who Is Responsible for Graduate Student Attrition—The Individual or the Institution? Toward an Explanation of the High and Persistent Rate of Attrition." Paper presented at the Annual Meeting of the American Education Research Association, New York, Apr. 9, 1996.

Lunnebord, C. E., and Lunnebord, P. W. "Doctoral Study Attrition in Psychology." *Research in Higher Education,* 1973, *1,* 379–387.

Malaney, G. D. "Differentiation in Graduate Education." *Research in Higher Education,* 1986, 25 (1), 82–96.

Malaney, G. D. "Graduate Education as an Area of Research in the Field of Higher Education." In J. C. Smart (ed.), *Higher Education: Handbook of Theory and Research,* Vol. 4. New York: Agathon Press, 1988.

Matthews, T. A., and Martin, D. J. "Reciprocal Suppression and Interaction Effects of Age with Undergraduate Grades and GRE on Graduate Performance in a College of Education." *Educational and Psychological Measurement,* 1992, *52,* 453–456.

Metzger, W. P. "Profession and Constitution: Two Definitions of Academic Freedom in America." *Texas Law Review,* 1988, *66,* 1265–1322.

Mitchell, K., Haynes, R., and Koenig, J. "Assessing the Validity of the Updated Medical College Admission Test." *Academic Medicine,* 1994, *69,* 394–401.

Mitler, M. L., and Bers, T. H. "Qualitative Assessment: An Institutional Reality Check." In T. H. Bers and M. L. Mitler (eds.), *Assessment and Testing: Myths and Realities.* New Directions for Community Colleges, no. 88. San Francisco: Jossey-Bass, 1994.

Morgan, D. L., Kearney, R. C., and Regens, J. L. "Assessing Quality Among Graduate Institutions of Higher Education in the United States." *Social Science Quarterly,* 1976, *57,* 670–679.

Morrison, T., and Morrison, M. "A Meta-Analytic Assessment of the Predictive Validity of the Quantitative and Verbal Components of the Graduate Record Examination with Graduate Grade Point Average Representing the Criterion of Graduate Success." *Educational and Psychological Measurement,* 1995, *55* (2), 309–316.

Morton, J. *Attrition of Graduate Students at the University of California, San Diego.* La Jolla: Office of Graduate Studies and Research, University of California, San Diego, 1976.

Mulvey, P. J., and Dodge, E. "Enrollments and Degrees Report." *AIP Report,* Jan. 1996.

Murphy, P. "Post-Graduate Degree No Guarantee of High Rate of Return in Job Market." *Pittsburgh Post-Gazette,* Aug. 17, 1993, p. B15.

Nairn, A., and Associates. *The Reign of ETS.* Washington, D.C.: Ralph Nader, 1980.

National Center for Education Statistics, U.S. Department of Education. *Degrees Conferred in Institutions of Higher Education, by Race/Ethnicity and Sex: 1976–77 through 1986–87.* Washington, D.C.: Government Printing Office, 1990.

National Center for Education Statistics, U.S. Department of Education. *Projection of Education Statistics to 2002.* Washington, D.C.: Government Printing Office, 1991.

National Center for Education Statistics, U.S. Department of Education. *1992–93 National Postsecondary Student Aid Study (NPSAS:93), Graduate Data Analysis System.* Washington, D.C.: Government Printing Office, 1993a.

National Center for Education Statistics, U.S. Department of Education. *Occupational and Educational Outcomes of Recent College Graduates One Year After Graduation: 1991 Contractor Report.* Washington, D.C.: Government Printing Office, 1993b.

National Center for Education Statistics, U.S. Department of Education. *Digest of Educational Statistics, 1995.* Washington, D.C.: Government Printing Office, 1995.

National Center for Education Statistics, U.S. Department of Education. Integrated Post-secondary Education System. "Completions," "Consolidated," and "Fall Enrollment" surveys, 1996.

National Research Council. *Survey of Earned Doctorates.* Washington, D.C.: National Academy Press, 1996.

National Science Foundation (NSF). *Human Resources for Science and Technology: The Asian Region.* Washington, D.C.: NSF, 1993.

Nerad, M. *Doctoral Education at the University of California and Factors Affecting Time to Degree.* Oakland, Calif.: University of California, Office of the President, 1991.

Nerad, M. "Using Time, Money, and Human Resources Efficiently and Effectively in the Case of Women Graduate Students." Paper prepared for the Conference Proceedings of "Science and Engineering Programs: On Target for Women?" Sponsored by the National Academy of Sciences/National Research Council/Office of Scientific and Engineering Personnel, 1992.

Nerad, M. "Beyond Traditional Modes of Mentoring: The University of California, Berkeley Approach." In *A Conversation About Mentoring: Trends and Models.* Washington D.C.: Council of Graduate Schools, 1995.

Nerad, M., and Cerny, J. "From Facts to Action: Expanding the Educational Role of the Graduate Division." *CGS Communicator* (special issue), May 1991.

Nerad, M., and Cerny, J. "From Facts to Action: Expanding the Educational Role of the Graduate Division." In L. L. Baird (ed.), *Increasing Graduate Student Retention and Degree Attainment.* New Directions for Institutional Research, no. 80. San Francisco: Jossey-Bass, 1993.

Nerad, M., and Stewart, C. "Assessing Doctoral Student Experience: Gender and Departmental Culture." Paper presented at the Annual Meeting of the Association for Institutional Research, San Francisco, May 26–29, 1991.

Nettles, M. T. *Black, Hispanic, and White Doctoral Students: Before, During, and After Enrolling in Graduate School. A Research Report of the Minority Graduate Education (MGE Project).* Princeton, N.J.: Educational Testing Service, 1990.

Nettles, M. T., and others. "Comparative and Predictive Analyses of Black and White Students' College Achievement and Experiences." *Journal of Higher Education,* 1986, 57 (3), 289–318.

Neuschatz, M., and Mulvey, P. J. "1994 Initial Employment Follow-Up of 1993 Physics Degree Recipients." *AIP Report,* July 1995.

Nora, A., and Cabrera, A. F. "Examining Graduate Education Through Structural Modeling." In L. L. Baird (ed.), *Increasing Graduate Student Retention and Degree Attainment.* New Directions for Institutional Research, no. 80. San Francisco: Jossey-Bass, 1993.

Nora, A., Cabrera, A. F., and Shinville, P. "Graduate Student Involvement in Scholarly Behavior: A Structural Model." Paper presented at the 1992 Annual Meeting of the American Educational Research Association, San Francisco, 1994.

Nyquist, J. D., and Wulff, D. H. *Working Effectively with Graduate Assistants.* Thousand Oaks, Calif.: Sage, 1996.

O'Brien, E. M. "Master's Degree Students and Recipients: A Profile." *ACE Research Briefs,* 1992, 3 (1).

Office for Minority Education. *An Approach for Identifying and Minimizing Bias in Standardized Tests: A Set of Guidelines.* Princeton, N.J.: Educational Testing Service, 1980.

Olivas, M. A. "Reflections on Professorial Academic Freedom: Second Thoughts on the Third 'Essential Freedom.'" *Stanford Law Review,* 1993, 45, 1835–1858.

Oliver, J., and Brown, L. B. "College and University Minority Recruitment: Barriers, Recruitment Principles and Design Guidelines." *Journal of College Student Development,* 1988, 29 (1), 40–47.

Oromaner, M. J. "A Note on Analytical Properties and Prestige of Sociology Departments." *American Sociologist,* 1970, 5, 240–244.

Pace, C. R. "Measuring the Quality of Student Effort." *Current Issues in Higher Education: Improving Teaching and Institutional Quality.* Washington, D.C.: American Association for Higher Education, 1980.

Pace, C. R. *Student Effort: A New Key to Assessing Quality.* Project on the Study of Quality in Undergraduate Education. Los Angeles: Higher Education Research Institute, University of California, 1986.

Pascarella, E. T., and Terenzini, P. T. *How College Affects Students.* San Francisco: Jossey-Bass, 1991.

Pennock-Roman, M. "New Directions for Research on Spanish-Language Tests and Test-Time Bias." In M. A. Olivas (ed.), *Latino College Students.* New York: Teachers College Press. 1986a.

Pennock-Roman, M. "Fairness in the Use of Tests of Selective Admission of Hispanics." In M. A. Olivas (ed.), *Latino College Students.* New York: Teachers College Press, 1986b.

Pennock-Roman, M. *Differences Among Racial and Ethnic Groups in Mean Scores on the GRE and SAT: Cross-Sectional Comparisons.* GRE Report 86–09. Princeton, N.J.: Educational Testing Service, 1990.

Ploskonka, J. "The Use of Retrospective National Data for Institutional Evaluation." In L. L. Baird (ed.), *Increasing Graduate Student Retention and Degree Attainment.* New Directions for Institutional Research, no. 80. San Francisco: Jossey-Bass, 1993.

Powers, D. E. *Text Anxiety and the GRE General Test.* GRE Board Professional Report 83–17P/ETS Research Report 86–45. Princeton, N.J.: Educational Testing Service. 1986.

Prus, J., and Johnson, R. "A Critical Review of Student Assessment Options." In T. H. Bers and M. L. Mitler (eds.), *Assessment and Testing: Myths and Realities.* New Directions for Community Colleges, no. 88. San Francisco: Jossey-Bass, 1994.

Radin, N., Benbenishty, R., and Leon, J. "Predictors of Success in a Social Work Doctoral Program." *Social Service Review, 1982, 56,* 640–658.

Regan-Smith, M. G. "Graduate School as a Professional Development Experience." *Journal of Staff Development, 1994, 15* (3), 54–57.

Ribak, R., and Littlefield, A. *Doctoral Student Attrition at the University of California, San Diego.* San Diego: Office of Graduate Studies, University of California, 1992.

Sanford, N. *Where Colleges Fail: A Study of the Student as a Person.* San Francisco: Jossey-Bass, 1968.

Sax, L. J., Astin, A. W., Korn, W. S., and Mahoney, K. M. *The American Freshman: National Norms for Fall 1995.* Los Angeles: Higher Education Research Institute, University of California, 1995.

Schilling, K., and Schilling, K. M. "Descriptive Approaches to Assessment: Moving Beyond Meeting Requirements to Making a Difference." In Commission on Institutions of Higher Education, North Central Association of Colleges and Schools (ed.), *A Collection of Papers on Self-Study and Institutional Improvement.* (98th annual meeting.) Chicago: North Central Association, 1993.

Shull, H. "Investing in Graduate Education—Who Invests? Who Benefits?" Proceedings of the Annual Meeting of the Council of Graduate Schools in the United States, Colorado Springs, Colo., Dec. 1–3, 1982.

Simmons, R. O., and Thurgood, D. H. *Summary Report 1994: Doctorate Recipients from United States Universities.* Washington, D.C.: National Academy Press, 1995.

Slate, A. *AGS: A History.* Austin, Tex.: Association of Graduate Schools in the Association of American Universities, 1994.

Smart, J. C., and Hagedorn, L. S. "Enhancing Professional Competencies in Graduate Education." *Review of Higher Education, 1994, 17,* 241–257.

Smith, P. *Killing the Spirit: Higher Education in America.* New York: Viking Penguin, 1990.

Sowell, T. *Preferential Policies: An International Perspective.* New York: William Morrow, 1989.

Stark, J. S., Lowther, M. A., and Hagerty, B.M.K. *Responsive Professional Education: Balancing Outcomes and Opportunities.* ASHE-ERIC Higher Education Report, no. 3. Washington, D.C.: Association for the Study of Higher Education, 1986.

Stark, J. S., and Thomas, A. (eds.). *Assessment and Program Evaluation.* Needham Heights, Mass.: Simon & Schuster Custom Publishing, 1994.

Stern, D. M., and Lambert, M. J. "Graduate Training in Psychotherapy: Are Therapy Outcomes Enhanced?" *Journal of Consulting and Clinical Psychology,* 1995, *63,* 182–196.

Sternberg, R. J. *Beyond IQ.* New York: Cambridge University Press, 1985.

Study Group on the Conditions of Excellence in American Higher Education. *Involvement in Learning: Realizing the Potential of American Higher Education.* Washington, D.C.: National Institute of Education, 1984.

Sweezy v *New Hampshire,* 354 U.S. 234 (1957).

Swinton, S. S. *The Predictive Validity of the Restructured GRE with Particular Attention to Older Students.* GRE Board Professional Report 83–25P/ETS Research Report 87–22. Princeton, N.J.: Educational Testing Service, 1987.

Sykes, C. *Profscam: Professors and the Demise of Higher Education.* Washington, D.C.: Regnery Gateway, 1988.

Syverson, P. D. "Profound Change Underway in Flow of International Students, Reports Opens Doors 1994–95." *CGS Communicator,* Feb. 1996, p. 7.

Syverson, P. D., and Welch, S. R. *Graduate Enrollment and Degrees: 1986 to 1994.* Washington, D.C.: Council of Graduate Schools, 1996.

Terenzini, P. T. "Assessment with Open Eyes: Pitfalls in Studying Student Outcomes." In J. S. Stark and A. Thomas (eds.), *Assessment and Program Evaluation.* Needham Heights, Mass.: Simon & Schuster Custom Publishing, 1994.

Terenzini, P. T., and Pascarella, E. T. "Living with Myths: Undergraduate Education in America." *Change,* 1994, *26,* 28–32.

Thacker, A. J., and Williams, R. E. "The Relationship of the Graduate Record Examination to Grade Point Averages and Success in Graduate School." *Educational and Psychological Measurement,* 1974, *34,* 934–944.

Thomas, B. E., Clewell, B. C., and Pearson, W., Jr. *The Role and Activities of American Graduate Schools in Recruiting, Enrolling and Retaining U.S. Black and Hispanic Students.* Princeton, N.J.: Educational Testing Service, 1992.

Tinto, V. *Leaving College: Rethinking the Causes and Cures of Student Attrition.* (2nd ed.) Chicago: University of Chicago Press, 1993.

Trent, W. T., and Copeland, E. J. *Effectiveness of State Financial Aid in the Production of Black Doctoral Recipients.* Atlanta, Ga.: Southern Education Foundation, 1987.

Tucker, A., Gottlieb, D., and Pease, J. *Factors Related to Attrition Among Doctoral Students.* East Lansing: Michigan State University, 1964.

Turner, C.S.V., and Thompson, J. R. "Socializing Women Doctoral Students: Minority and Majority Experiences." *Review of Higher Education,* 1993, *16* (3), 355–370.

Vaseleck, J. "Stop Working and Put Down Your Pencils: The Use and Misuse of Standardized Admission Tests." *Journal of College and University Law,* 1994, *20* (4), 405–415.

Webster, D. S. "Advantages and Disadvantages of Methods of Assessing Quality." *Change,* Oct. 1981, *13,* 20–24.

Webster, D. S. *Academic Quality Rankings of American Colleges and Universities.* Springfield, Ill.: Charles C. Thomas, 1986a.

Webster, D. S. "Ranking Academic Quality." *Change,* 1986b, *18,* 34–41.

Webster, D. S. "Reputational Rankings of Colleges, Universities, and Individual Disciplines and Fields of Study, from Their Beginnings to the Present." In J. C. Smart (ed.), *Higher Education: Handbook of Theory and Research,* Vol. 8. New York: Agathon Press, 1992.

Wergin, J. F. (ed.). *Using Consultants Successfully.* New Directions for Higher Education, no. 73. San Francisco: Jossey-Bass, 1991.

Wilkinson, R. K. "For 1993, Doctoral Scientists and Engineers Report 1.6 Percent Unemployment Rate But 4.3 Percent Underemployment." *Data Brief,* 1995, (5).

Williamson, M. J., and Fenske, R. H. "Mexican American and American Indian Students' Satisfaction with their Doctoral Programs." In S. Hood and H. T. Frierson, Jr. (eds.), *Beyond the Dream: Meaningful Program Evaluation and Assessment to Achieve Equal Opportunities for Minorities in Higher Education.* Greenwich, Conn.: JAI Press, 1993.

Willie, C. V., Grady, M. K., and Hope, R. O. *African-Americans and the Doctoral Experience: Implications for Policy.* New York: Teachers College Press, 1991.

Willingham, W. W., Lewis, C., Morgan, R., and Ramist, L. *Predicting College Grades.* New York: College Board and Educational Testing Service, 1990.

Wilson, K. M. *A Study of the Validity of the Restructured GRE Aptitude Test for Predicting First-Year Performance in Graduate Study.* GRE Board Research Report 78–6R/ETS Research Report 82–34. Princeton, N.J.: Educational Testing Service, 1982.

Wingspread Group on Higher Education. *An American Imperative: Higher Expectations for Higher Education.* Racine, Wis.: Johnson Foundation, 1993.

Wright, W. A., and Associates. *Teaching Improvement Practices: Successful Strategies for Higher Education.* Bolton, Mass.: Aiken Press, 1995.

INDEX

ORDERING INFORMATION

NEW DIRECTIONS FOR INSTITUTIONAL RESEARCH is a series of paperback books that provides planners and administrators in all types of academic institutions with guidelines in such areas as resource coordination, information analysis, program evaluation, and institutional management. Books in the series are published quarterly in spring, summer, fall, and winter and are available for purchase by subscription as well as by single copy.

SUBSCRIPTIONS cost $52.00 for individuals (a savings of 35 percent over single-copy prices) and $79.00 for institutions, agencies, and libraries. Please do not send institutional checks for personal subscriptions. Standing orders are accepted.

SINGLE COPIES cost $20.00 plus shipping (see below) when payment accompanies order. California, New Jersey, New York, and Washington, D.C., residents please include appropriate sales tax. Canadian residents add GST and any local taxes. Billed orders will be charged shipping and handling. No billed shipments to post office boxes. Orders from outside the United States or Canada *must be prepaid* in U.S. dollars or charged to VISA, MasterCard, or American Express.

SHIPPING (SINGLE COPIES ONLY): $10.00 and under, add $2.50; $10.01–$20, add $3.50; $20.01–$50, add $4.50; $50.01–$75, add $5.50; $75.01–$100, add $6.50; $100.01–$150, add $7.50; over $150, add $8.50. Outside of North America, please add $15.00 per book for priority shipment.

DISCOUNTS FOR QUANTITY ORDERS are available. Please write to the address below for information.

ALL ORDERS must include either the name of an individual or an official purchase order number. Please submit your order as follows:
   Subscriptions: specify series and year subscription is to begin
   Single copies: include individual title code (such as IR78)

MAIL ALL ORDERS TO:
   Jossey-Bass Publishers
   350 Sansome Street
   San Francisco, CA 94104-1342

FOR SUBSCRIPTION SALES OUTSIDE OF THE UNITED STATES, CONTACT:
any international subscription agency or Jossey-Bass directly.

UNITED STATES POSTAL SERVICE™

Statement of Ownership, Management, and Circulation
(Required by 39 U.S.C. 3685)

1. Publication Title	2. Publication No.	3. Filing Date
NEW DIRECTIONS FOR INSTITUTIONAL RESEARCH	0 2 7 1 - 0 5 7 9	9/26/96

4. Issue Frequency	5. No. of Issues Published Annually	6. Annual Subscription Price
QUARTERLY	4	$52 - indiv. $79 - instit.

7. Complete Mailing Address of Known Office of Publication *(Street, City, County, State, and ZIP+4) (Not Printer)*

350 SANSOME STREET, SAN FRANCISCO, CA 94104 (SAN FRANCISCO COUNTY)

8. Complete Mailing Address of Headquarters or General Business Office of Publisher *(Not Printer)*

SAME AS ABOVE

9. Full Names and Complete Mailing Addresses of Publisher, Editor, and Managing Editor *(Do Not Leave Blank)*

Publisher *(Name and Complete Mailing Address)*

JOSSEY-BASS INC., PUBLISHERS (SEE ABOVE ADDRESS)

Editor *(Name and Complete Mailing Address)*

J. FREDRICKS VOLKWEIN, DIRECTOR OF INSTITUTIONAL RESEARCH, SUNY ALBANY, ADMINISTRATION 241, ALBANY, NY 12222

Managing Editor *(Name and Complete Mailing Address)*

NONE

10. Owner *(If owned by a corporation, its name and address must be stated and also immediately thereafter the names and addresses of stockholders owning or holding 1 percent or more of the total amount of stock. If not owned by a corporation, give the names and addresses of the individual owners must be given. If owned by a partnership or other unincorporated firm, its name and address as well as that of each individual must be given. If the publication is published by a nonprofit organization, its name and address must be stated.) (Do Not Leave Blank.)*

Full Name	Complete Mailing Address
SIMON & SCHUSTER INC.	P.O. BOX 1172
	ENGLEWOOD CLIFFS, NH 07632-1172

11. Known Bondholders, Mortgagees, and Other Security Holders Owning or Holding 1 Percent or More of Total Amount of Bonds, Mortgages, or Other Securities. If none, check here. ☐ None

Full Name	Complete Mailing Address
(SAME AS ABOVE)	(SAME AS ABOVE)

12. For completion by nonprofit organizations authorized to mail at special rates. The purpose, function, and nonprofit status of this organization and the exempt status for federal income tax purposes: *(Check one)*
☐ Has Not Changed During Preceding 12 Months
☐ Has Changed During Preceding 12 Months
(If changed, publisher must submit explanation of change with this statement)

PS Form 3526, October 1994   *(See Instructions on Reverse)*

---

13. Publication Name	14. Issue Date for Circulation Data Below
NEW DIRECTIONS FOR INSTIT. RESEARCH	WINTER 1995

15. Extent and Nature of Circulation	Average No. Copies Each Issue During Preceding 12 Months	Actual No. Copies of Single Issue Published Nearest to Filing Date
a. Total No. Copies *(Net Press Run)*	1999	2052
b. Paid and/or Requested Circulation (1) Sales Through Dealers and Carriers, Street Vendors, and Counter Sales *(Not Mailed)*	435	459
(2) Paid or Requested Mail Subscriptions *(Include Advertisers' Proof Copies/Exchange Copies)*	871	883
c. Total Paid and/or Requested Circulation *(Sum of 15a(1) and 15a(2))*	1306	1342
d. Free Distribution by Mail *(Samples, Complimentary, and Other Free)*	75	75
e. Free Distribution Outside the Mail *(Carriers or Other Means)*	0	0
f. Total Free Distribution *(Sum of 15d and 15e)*	75	75
g. Total Distribution *(Sum of 15c and 15f)*	1381	1417
h. Copies Not Distributed (1) Office Use, Leftovers, Spoiled	618	635
(2) Return from News Agents	0	0
i. Total *(Sum of 15g, 15h(1), and 15h(2))*	1999	2052
Percent Paid and/or Requested Circulation *(15c / 15g x 100)*	95%	95%

16. This Statement of Ownership will be printed in the WINTER 1996 issue of this publication. ☐ Check box if not required to publish.

17. Signature and Title of Editor, Publisher, Business Manager, or Owner

Susan F. Lewis   SUSAN E. LEWIS, PERIODICALS DIRECTOR   Date 9/26/96

I certify that all information furnished on this form is true and complete. I understand that anyone who furnishes false or misleading information on this form or who omits material or information requested on the form may be subject to criminal sanctions *(including fines and imprisonment)* and/or civil sanctions *(including multiple damages and civil penalties)*.

Instructions to Publishers

1. Complete and file one copy of this form with your postmaster on or before October 1, annually. Keep a copy of the completed form for your records.

2. Include in items 10 and 11, in cases where the stockholder or security holder is a trustee, the name of the person or corporation for whom the trustee is acting. Also include the names and addresses of individuals who are stockholders who own or hold 1 percent or more of the total amount of bonds, mortgages, or other securities of the publishing corporation. In item 11, if none, check box. Use blank sheets if more space is required.

3. Be sure to furnish all information called for in item 15, regarding circulation. Free circulation must be shown in items 15d, e, and f.

4. If the publication had second-class authorization as a general or requester publication, this Statement of Ownership, Management, and Circulation must be published; it must be printed in any issue in October or the first printed issue after October, if the publication is not published during October.

5. In item 16, indicate date of the issue in which this Statement of Ownership will be printed.

6. Item 17 must be signed.

Failure to file or publish a statement of ownership may lead to suspension of second-class authorization.

PS Form 3526, October 1994 *(Reverse)*